Reading Skills
5–6

Written by
Trisha Callella

Editor: Carla Hamaguchi
Illustrator: Corbin Hillam
Designer/Production: Moonhee Pak/Carrie Rickmond
Cover Designer: Barbara Peterson
Art Director: Tom Cochrane
Project Director: Carolea Williams

Table of Contents

Introduction 4

Figurative Language
Unfinished Words 5
Puzzling Proverbs. 6
Sensational Similes. 7
What Are You Talking About? 8
You've Got to Be Kidding! 9
In the News 10

Homophones
Homophones 11
Puzzled? 12
All Mixed Up 13
Missing Words 14

Synonyms and Antonyms
Thinking Out of the Box 15
In Other Words 16
Synonym Sandwiches. 17
That's Not What I Said. 18
Antonym Match-Up. 19
Opposites Attract. 20

Analogies
Secret Code 21
Match It Up 22
Unscramble It! 23
Analyze This! 24

Vocabulary
Fill In the Blanks. 25
What Does It Mean? 26
Sentence Sense. 27
You Be the Dictionary 28
Prefix Match-Up. 29

Question Comprehension
Personal Opinion Questions 30
Are You Serious? 31
Always, Sometimes, Never 32
You're the Teacher. 33
You're the Teacher Again 34

Interpreting Written Directions
Marshmallow Cereal Bars 35
Handy Dandy Card Holder 36
What's the Answer? 37
Hawaiian Pizza. 38

Categorization
Four in Four 39
Elimination. 40
A Full House 41
The Outline 42
What Category?. 43

Main Idea
The Big Idea. 44
How Supportive Are You?. 45
Prove It! 46
Main Idea and Details 47

Predicting
Paired Up 48
Get Logical! 49
Predictions Aren't Perfect 50
Television Titles 51

Characterization
Get to Know the Character. 52
Casting Call. 53
A Feel for the Character 54
Traits on Plates. 55

Setting
Matching Settings 56
Get in the Mood 57
It's in the Details 58
Ready on the Set 59

Sequencing
What's Next? 60
Sequence Your Life 61
Comics 62
The Life of Bill Gates 63

Context Clues
Which Meaning Makes Sense? 64
Not So Tricky After All. 65
Get to the Root of the Matter 66
Context Clues Crossword. 67
Context Clues 68

Cause and Effect
Why Did It Happen? 69
What Happened?. 70
What and Why? 71
The Good and the Bad of It All 72

Find the Cause or Effect 73

Fact and Opinion
Alluring Advertisements 74
Unscrambled Hints. 75
For Sale 76
The Flip Side. 77

Summarizing
Key Points 78
Big Ideas of a Summary. 79
Comical Summaries 80
Summarize Anything. 81

Plot
Plot Parts 82
Conflicts 83
Plot It Out 84
Turning Points 85

Problem and Solution
What's the Problem?. 86
I've Got It! 87
Solving Problems 88
On the Other Hand 89

Reasoning
Inconsistencies 90
Name It! 91
Please Explain. 92
Is It Reasonable? 93

Compare and Contrast
Alike or Different. 94
Amazing Animal Similarities. 95
As Different as Night and Day 96

Making Connections
Personal Connections 97
What in the World?. 98
Connect the Dots. 99

Theme
The Best Choice 100
Author Messages 101
Name That Theme 102
Topic or Theme?. 103

Structural Features
Poetry 104
Features of Literature 105
Lear's Limericks 106
Positively Poetic 107

Organized Comprehension
Sort It Out 108
Get Organized 109
Catch Phrases 110
Acronyms 111

Inferences
Name That Activity 112
What Do You Think?. 113
Cartoon Capers 114
Favorite Sports. 115
What's Next? 116

Answer Key 117

Introduction

Each book in the Power Practice™ series contains over 100 ready-to-use activity pages to provide students with skill practice. The fun activities can be used to supplement and enhance what you are teaching in your classroom. Give an activity page to students as independent class work, or send the pages home as homework to reinforce skills taught in class. An answer key is provided for quick reference.

The practical and creative activities in the reading skills books provide the perfect practice with over 20 reading skills. Each book is divided into sections covering these various skills.

Reading Skills 5–6 provides activities that will directly assist students in practicing and reinforcing skills such as
- inferences
- drawing conclusions
- context clues
- sequencing
- predicting
- making connections
- figurative language
- main idea
- summarizing
- cause and effect
- point of view

Use these ready-to-go activities to "recharge" skill review and give students the power to succeed!

Name _____ Date _____

Unfinished Words

FIGURATIVE LANGUAGE

> An **idiom** is a form of figurative language where the meaning of the phrase cannot be inferred from the meanings of the words that make it up.
> Example: She has a heart of gold.
> Her heart is not literally made of gold. This idiom is a more colorful way of saying that she is kind.

Complete each sentence by choosing the best idiom from the list below.

hit the sack	sleep on it
raining cats and dogs	in hot water
blow your top	brush up on
fit like a glove	on the ball
up to something	

1 Her mom said, "It's getting late. It's time for you to _____."

2 If you get into trouble, then you know you're _____.

3 The man told the shoe salesman that the new boots _____.

4 Before going to France, she decided to _____ her French so she could speak to the people and understand them.

5 Sometimes when people can't decide what to do, they _____ and decide in the morning.

6 Her little brother had mud on his face and hands. She knew he was

_____ when he was out in the garden.

7 The storm was so bad that it was _____.

8 Have you ever gotten so upset that you thought you would

_____?

9 Wow! She figured that out so fast! That girl is really _____.

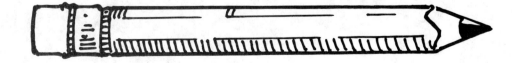

Name _____ Date _____

Puzzling Proverbs

Figurative Language

A **proverb** is a short saying that has been around for a long time. Proverbs are a form of figurative language that makes sentences sound more colorful and interesting. Like idioms, they cannot be interpreted literally.

Example: An apple a day keeps the doctor away.

That doesn't literally mean that you will avoid doctors by eating apples daily. It's a colorful way of saying that eating fresh fruit is a healthy choice.

Fill in the crossword puzzle by completing the proverbs.

Across
1. No _____ is good news.
3. A rolling _____ gathers no moss.
4. All work and no play makes Jack a _____ boy.
6. The _____ bird catches the worm.
7. A fool and his money are soon _____.
8. _____ killed the cat.
9. Beauty is only _____ deep.
11. Don't judge a book by its _____.

Down
2. Like father, like _____.
3. A penny _____ is a penny earned.
5. Actions speak _____ than words.
7. While the cat's away, the mice will _____.
8. Beggars can't be _____.
10. Every cloud has a _____ lining.

Reading Skills • 5-6 © 2004 Creative Teaching Press

Name _____ Date _____

Sensational Similes

FIGURATIVE LANGUAGE

A **simile** is a form of figurative language that uses the words *like* or *as* to compare people, events, or objects.
   Example: Her face was as red as an apple when she found out her son didn't turn in his report on time.
   That's a figurative way of saying she was very angry.

Use your own words to complete each simile.

1. Her voice was as loud as a _____.

2. That basketball player is as tall as a _____.

3. His little sister was as annoying as a _____.

4. His dry legs felt like _____.

5. The sky is as colorful as a _____.

6. She was slow like _____.

7. She has cheeks like _____.

8. The cave was as dark as a _____.

9. The work was as hard as _____.

10. My new sports car is as fast as a _____.

11. He ate like a _____.

12. That pizza was as spicy as a _____.

13. His shoes were as smelly as a _____.

14. The clouds were fluffy like _____.

15. Sometimes she thought her mom was as stubborn as a _____.

16. The floor was slippery like _____.

Reading Skills • 5-6 © 2004 Creative Teaching Press

Name _____   Date _____

What Are You Talking About?

FIGURATIVE LANGUAGE

Personification is used in books when the author wants to give human characteristics to animals or objects. You've read it many times in animal fantasies and traditional fiction.
Example: "The aged mouse simply smiled in appreciation for the kind words he had heard." Mice don't really smile, so that's a human characteristic the author is trying to apply to the mouse character.

Underline the use of personification in each sentence. Then explain its true meaning on the line.

1 The whale sang with glee when he was released into the open sea.

_____

2 Her homework was calling her name.

_____

3 The water danced around the boat in the storm.

_____

4 The glasses were begging to be worn.

_____

5 She was awakened from a deep sleep when the night wind knocked on her window.

_____

6 The trash truck opened its mouth and swallowed the newspapers whole.

_____

Reading Skills • 5-6 © 2004 Creative Teaching Press

Name _____ Date _____

You've Got to Be Kidding!

FIGURATIVE LANGUAGE

Hyperbole is an expression of exaggeration that authors use to make characters or situations much bigger or smaller than they really are.

Underline the use of hyperbole in each sentence. Then explain its true meaning on the line.

1 Robert cried a river of tears when he watched that movie.

_____

2 I've told you a million times not to exaggerate!

_____

3 Dawn was so tired that she could sleep for a year!

_____

4 She said, "These boxes weigh a ton!"

_____

5 It'll take her all day just to find her desk.

_____

6 She wears so much makeup that you can't tell where her face begins or ends!

_____

7 The town where I grew up is so isolated that even insects won't live there!

_____

8 Her daughter said, " I think of you a thousand times a day!"

_____

9 Our library is so old, that the books have Roman numerals for page numbers!

_____

10 By the time I finish this garden, I'll be a hundred years old!

_____

Reading Skills • 5-6 © 2004 Creative Teaching Press

In the News

FIGURATIVE LANGUAGE

A **simile** uses the words *like* or *as* to compare people, events, or objects.
Personification is used when the author wants to give human characteristics to animals or objects.
Hyperbole is an expression of exaggeration to make characters or situations much bigger or smaller than they really are.

Read the newspaper article below. Look for the three types of figurative language. When you find an example, underline it and label it according to the following key: **H** = hyperbole, **S** = simile, **P** = personification.

IN THE NEWS

The Streak Is Over

Can you believe it? The Whales were at it again this weekend! We thought the losing streak would go on forever!

Luckily, the Weaver Whales came through with flying colors. They were off to a running start early in the first quarter with Charlesworth leading the game in three point shooting. They were as organized as a teacher's desk! They had the other team spinning in their shoes as if they didn't know what hit them. Arias was as powerful as a lion, while Olson was as sly as a fox. Before anyone knew it, they were tossing that ball right through the hoop. The hoop was even cheering on the team the way it swayed back and forth.

By half time, the Whales were 15 points ahead of their most difficult opponents—the Lee Leopards. However, the Whales proved that they were too hot to handle in the third quarter. In fact, the coach of the Leopards got pretty steamed up. You could hear his yelling all the way to Japan!

Hankin was particularly impressive when he ran as quick as lightning across the court and planted the ball straight into the basket. What a dunk! If it were a doughnut, the coffee would have spilled everywhere! You could almost hear the ball begging for a rest.

The Whales were leading the way right to the last buzzer. The writing was on the wall. Their three-game losing streak was finally over! They were ready to resume their place at the top. Once again, the Weaver Whales were making waves. This time without the storm. It looks like sunny days are here again!

Reading Skills • 5-6 © 2004 Creative Teaching Press

Homophones

HOMOPHONES

The word **homophone** literally means "same sound." Homophones are words that sound the same but are spelled differently.
Examples:
night and knight
hair and hare

Unscramble the homophone for each word.

1. there _____ (terih)

2. band _____ (ndnabe)

3. blue _____ (webl)

4. bored _____ (oabdr)

5. sell _____ (lelc)

6. tale _____ (aitl)

7. waist _____ (astwe)

8. forth _____ (torfuh)

9. seem _____ (smea)

10. horse _____ (roshae)

11. packed _____ (pcta)

12. piece _____ (eepac)

13. peer _____ (iepr)

14. which _____ (twchi)

15. peek _____ (kaep)

Puzzled?

HOMOPHONES

Fill in the crossword puzzle with the correct spelling of the correct homophone based on the context of the sentences. Use the words from the box for help.

plane	plain	knight	night	wait	weight
steak	stake	sweet	suite	peddle	pedal
which	witch	there	their	sealing	ceiling

Across

1. I flew on a _____.
2. Is that _____ well done?
3. He pushed the _____ into the ground.
4. At _____, the stars are amazing.
5. These cookies taste so _____.
6. The doctor had me use a scale to check my _____.
7. _____ one did you choose?
8. Is it the house over _____?

Down

1. That salesman is trying to _____ his vitamins.
3. He had trouble _____ the package so he got tape.
5. Would you like the honeymoon _____?
9. He did not _____ for me; he just left.
10. The _____ in armor sat on the horse.
11. The main character is an evil, wicked _____.
12. Where is _____ box of cookies? They can't find them anywhere.

Reading Skills • 5-6 © 2004 Creative Teaching Press

All Mixed Up

HOMOPHONES

> **Homophones** are words that sound the same but are spelled differently.
>   Examples:
>   blew and blue
>   hear and here

Read the sentences. Cross out the homophones that are used incorrectly. Write the correct word above each incorrect one.

1 Her ant blue her a kiss goodbye as she climbed on bored the plain.

2 The farmer tried to hall a heavy load of hey onto his tractor, but he mist.

3 The boy pulled a mussel when he bent down to pick the beautiful flours.

4 In the mourning, she always had trouble deciding witch dress to ware.

5 He asked his teacher if their wood be a test the next day.

6 They lost there calculators and couldn't fined them.

7 The hair ran threw the bushes trying to hide from the dog.

8 She couldn't eat for several days so she lost a lot of wait!

9 He didn't know weather to run or walk.

10 The man thought he mite eat stake for dinner that knight.

Reading Skills • 5–6 © 2004 Creative Teaching Press

Missing Words

HOMOPHONES

Use a word from the box to complete each sentence with the correct homophone.

herd	hear	new	chili	hire	knew	oar	reign
hole	higher	rain	here	ore	whole	chilly	heard

1 I hope it doesn't _____ on our parade.

2 When will the king finish his _____?

3 Can you please bring me the other _____ for the canoe?

4 The mine produced a great deal of _____.

5 Which candidate did you _____ for the job?

6 We watched the hot air balloon go even _____ into the sky.

7 I just _____ the news!

8 He has a _____ of buffalo on his ranch.

9 Is that a _____ in your sock?

10 Can you believe he ate that _____ doughnut in one bite?

11 I can't _____ you. Please speak up.

12 Come over _____!

13 I _____ I could count on you!

14 Is that a _____ sweater? I've never seen it before.

15 It was _____ outside so I put on my jacket.

16 I put some _____ and onions on my hot dog.

Reading Skills • 5-6 © 2004 Creative Teaching Press

Thinking Out of the Box

SYNONYMS AND ANTONYMS

Synonyms are words that have the same meaning.
Example: thrilled and excited   They both mean that someone is very happy.

Each package has a word on it. Add four synonyms for each word to make the package complete.

similar

hilarious

solicit

duplicate

challenging

query

disrupt

cordial

evil

Name _____ Date _____

In Other Words . . .

Synonyms are words that have the same meaning.   Example: difficult and challenging

---

Read each sentence. Circle the best synonym for the underlined word.

1 Luis became <u>agitated</u> when his brother wouldn't open the door and let him in.
  irritated   ecstatic   bothersome   friendly

2 Are you <u>satisfied</u> with your grade in reading?
  disappointed   confused   pleased   dejected

3 The Olsons <u>reside</u> on a large ranch in the northern part of the state.
  help   ride   work   live

4 Remember to reread your writing to search for <u>errors</u> before turning in your story.
  synonyms   adjectives   initials   mistakes

5 The tornado <u>demolished</u> the trees and homes in its path.
  deserted   constructed   destroyed   rebuilt

6 Matt closed his mouth <u>abruptly</u> before letting the secret out.
  tightly   late   quickly   softly

7 The two sisters <u>argued</u> over who would get to go first in the game.
  bickered   voted   decided   snickered

8 There was a "For Sale" sign on the lawn of the <u>vacant</u> house.
  remodeled   empty   haunted   immaculate

9 Remember to end every paragraph with a <u>concluding</u> sentence.
  finishing   beginning   descriptive   revised

10 Two parents chose to <u>accompany</u> the class on their field trip.
  divide   lead   continue   escort

11 Ashley <u>despises</u> people who are cruel to their pets.
  detests   encourages   dismisses   ignores

12 Joey was <u>fascinated</u> by palindromes—words and numbers that are the same in each direction.
  annoyed   distracted   excited   bored

Reading Skills • 5-6 © 2004 Creative Teaching Press

Synonym Sandwiches

SYNONYMS AND ANTONYMS

Complete each sandwich by writing two synonyms for each word. Use words from the word box.

hilarious	appreciative	detrimental	cool
amount	agitate	picked	irritate
accompany	grateful	meet	gigantic
disappeared	funny	dissipated	dangerous
total	enormous	selected	nippy

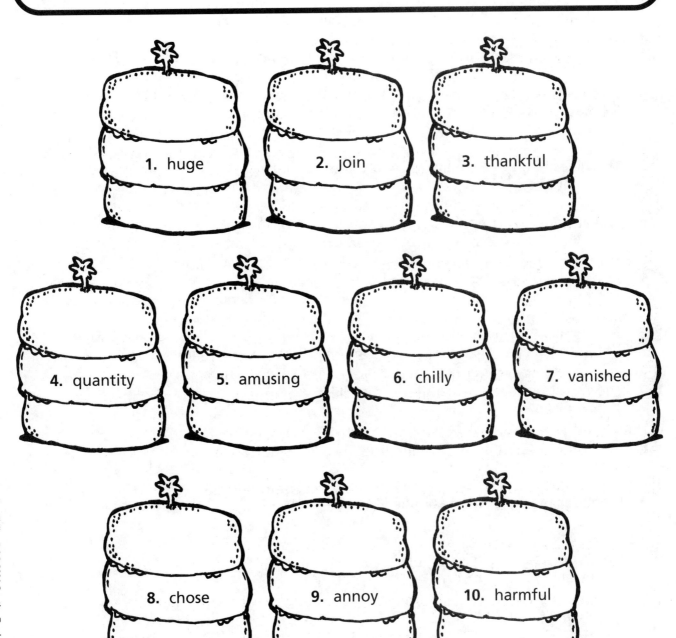

1. huge

2. join

3. thankful

4. quantity

5. amusing

6. chilly

7. vanished

8. chose

9. annoy

10. harmful

That's Not What I Said

SYNONYMS AND ANTONYMS

Antonyms are words that have opposite meanings.
Example: easy and hard   The word *easy* means exactly the opposite of the word *hard*.

Read each sentence. Circle the best antonym for the underlined word.

1 The bus <u>departs</u> at 11:50 a.m.
    leaves   arrives   opens   stops

2 Melissa is <u>confident</u> that she will wear toe shoes by next month.
    unsure   careful   hopeful   positive

3 Salvador was <u>disappointed</u> with his poor math grades.
    sad   angry   pleased   unsure

4 The hiker had to carefully <u>descend</u> the mountain.
    climb   locate   navigate   depart

5 The antique toy chest was very <u>sturdy</u>.
    tough   rugged   fragile   filthy

6 Joseph <u>discovered</u> his love of music.
    found   ended   lost   enjoyed

7 The lights <u>abruptly</u> went out.
    quickly   suddenly   slowly   carefully

8 The forest was very <u>peaceful</u> for Micaela.
    frightening   calming   quiet   beautiful

9 She tried to <u>conceal</u> the picture.
    show   hide   take   sell

10 Is your dog as <u>energetic</u> as mine?
    happy   playful   lazy   hungry

11 Does your teacher smile <u>often</u>?
    rarely   nicely   quickly   sometimes

12 Have you <u>completed</u> your personal narrative?
    started   acceptable   finished   edited

Reading Skills • 5-6 © 2004 Creative Teaching Press

Antonym Match-Up

SYNONYMS AND ANTONYMS

Match each word to its antonym. Write the letter of the antonym on the line.

_____ **1** ignorant

_____ **2** expensive

_____ **3** cowardly

_____ **4** separated

_____ **5** lenient

_____ **6** organized

_____ **7** rewarded

_____ **8** decayed

_____ **9** unique

_____ **10** generous

_____ **11** inaccurate

_____ **12** promptly

_____ **13** angry

_____ **14** exhausted

_____ **15** hinder

a. happy

b. strict

c. ordinary

d. joined

e. cheap

f. energized

g. punished

h. brave

i. belatedly

j. selfish

k. correct

l. fresh

m. messy

n. intelligent

o. help

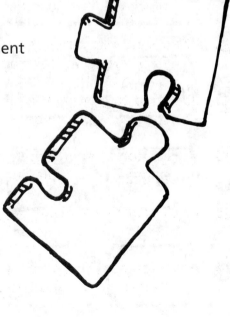

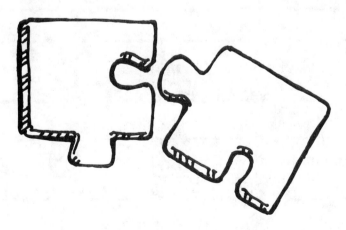

Opposites Attract

SYNONYMS AND ANTONYMS

Antonyms are like batteries—opposites attract. The more antonyms you can think of, the more voltage you will create. Write antonyms for the word in each row of batteries.

1 courteous

2 start

3 new

4 break

5 inquire

6 unsure

7 appear

8 leave

Reading Skills • 5-6 © 2004 Creative Teaching Press

Secret Code

ANALOGIES

A **synonym analogy** is one in which the two pairs of words are synonyms and you are to determine the missing synonym.
   Example: initiate : begin : : help : assist

Use a word from the box to complete each analogy. Think about the synonym relationship.

1 lawyer : attorney : : ___ ___ ___ ___ ___ ___ : physician
　　　　　　　　　　　　　　　　　2

2 happy : joyful : : courteous : ___ ___ ___ ___ ___ ___
　　　　　　　　　　　　　　　　　　　　8

3 nudge : push : : ponder : ___ ___ ___ ___ ___
　　　　　　　　　　　　　　　　　　　　6

thirsty	complain
draw	boring
friend	think
stop	doctor
polite	construct
gullible	relaxing

4 calm : ___ ___ ___ ___ ___ ___ ___ ___ : : speedy : fast
　　　　　　　11

5 chase : pursue : : cease : ___ ___ ___ ___
　　　　　　　　　　　　　　　　　12

6 gripe : ___ ___ ___ ___ ___ ___ ___ ___ : : cry : sob
　　　　　　　4　　　　　　　　5

7 embellish : decorate : : build : ___ ___ ___ ___ ___ ___ ___ ___ ___
　　　　　　　　　　　　　　　　　　　　　　　　　3

8 alter : change : : ___ ___ ___ ___ : illustrate
　　　　　　　　　　　　　　13

9 enemy : foe : : ___ ___ ___ ___ ___ ___ : pal
　　　　　　　　　　　　　　　　　7

10 eccentric : odd : : credulous : ___ ___ ___ ___ ___ ___ ___ ___
　　　　　　　　　　　　　　　　　　　　　10

11 dull : ___ ___ ___ ___ ___ ___ ___ : : funny : witty
　　　　　　　　　　　　　9

12 thin : gaunt : : parched : ___ ___ ___ ___ ___ ___ ___
　　　　　　　　　　　　　　　　　　　　1

What is the secret code? To solve it, write the letter from the analogies above on the correct numbered line.

___ ___ ___　___ ___ ___　___ ___　___ ___ ___ ___ ___ ___ ___ ___ ___ ___
 1　2　3　 4　5　6　 7　2　 5　6　5　8　2　9　10　11　12

___ ___ ___ ___ !
13　11　8　8

Match It Up

ANALOGIES

An **antonym analogy** is one in which the two pairs of words are antonyms and you are to determine the missing antonym.

Example: begin : end   : : open : close

Use a word from the word box to complete each analogy. Think about their opposite relationship.

cheerful	filthy	energized	novice	common
courage	purchase	hoard	fair	tiresome
microscopic	allow	untruthful	foolish	starve

1 true : false : : _____ : unjust

2 rich : poor : : _____ : clean

3 tired : _____ : : empty : full

4 ask : respond : : _____ : enormous

5 eat : _____ : : copy : originate

6 take : offer : : sell : _____

7 unique : _____ : : ocean : desert

8 hinder : help : : _____ : deny

9 fear : _____ : : unhappiness : joy

10 skeptic : believer : : _____ : professional

11 smart : _____ : : cold : hot

12 donate : _____ : : create : destroy

13 hopeful : discouraged : : _____ : honest

14 pleased : disappointed : : _____ : depressed

15 cloudy : sunny : : _____ : exciting

Name _____ Date _____

Unscramble It!

A **part-to-whole analogy** is one in which one word is a part or piece of the other.
   Example: toe : foot : : star : galaxy
   A toe is a part of a foot just like a star is a part of a galaxy.

Unscramble the missing word to complete these part-to-whole analogies.

1 month : _____ : : nose : face   (ryae)

2 fungus : spore : : _____ : computer   (bdrkyeoa)

3 salutation : _____ : : chapter : book   (rttlee)

4 player : team : : _____ : army   (rsoeild)

5 _____ : judicial branch : : president : executive branch   (eempusr ructo)

6 radius : _____ : : ray : line   (meeairtd)

7 brass instruments : _____ : : tree : forest   (stoaercrh)

8 sheep : _____ : : fish : school   (okflc)

9 letter : alphabet : : _____ : poem   (anzsat)

10 leaf : _____ : : tail : dog   (tpnal)

11 verb : _____ : : zip code : address   (csteeenn)

12 bird : flock : : wolf : _____   (kcpa)

13 _____ : pants : : pencil : eraser   (bowaerrd)

14 _____ : bathroom : : stove : kitchen   (ltteio)

15 _____ : football team : : point guard : basketball team   (kbqtucarrea)

Name _____ Date _____

Analyze This!

ANALOGIES

> A **characteristic analogy** is one in which one word is a characteristic of the other.
> Example: sour : lemon : : sweet : strawberry
> A lemon tastes sour just like a strawberry tastes sweet.
> The characteristic being compared is taste.

Complete each analogy with the missing word.

1. red : _____ : : green : emerald

2. happy : lark : : _____ : fox

3. yellow : sunflower : : _____ : gardenia

4. snake : slither : : _____ : fly

5. chef : _____ : : court reporter : transcript

6. rink : icy : : _____ : wet

7. _____ : malodorous : : flower : aromatic

8. _____ : benefactor : : malevolent : tyrant

9. desert : arid : : rain forest : _____

10. actor : _____ : : singer : choir

11. grain : silo : : _____ : coop

12. _____ : cinema : : orchestra : symphony

13. yoga : _____ : : dollar : currency

14. sailor : _____ : : astronaut : space shuttle

15. sheep : flock : : _____ : school

16. vaccine : _____ : : medicine : treatment

Reading Skills • 5-6 © 2004 Creative Teaching Press

Name _____ Date _____

Fill In the Blanks

VOCABULARY

Choose the word that best completes the sentence. Circle your answers.

The president of the United States is elected to a four- __1__ term in office. While in office, the president __2__ in the White House in Washington, D.C. Presidential elections take place every fourth November. In 1951, the 22nd Amendment to the Constitution was approved; this amendment provided that no person can be elected to the __3__ for more than two times. In order to be a __4__ for the presidency, the Constitution states that a person must be a natural-born American __5__, must be at least thirty-five years old, and must have lived in __6__ for at least fourteen years.

1 a. hour
   b. day
   c. decade
   d. year

2 a. resides
   b. soars
   c. stands
   d. camps

3 a. legislature
   b. military
   c. presidency
   d. Supreme Court

4 a. person
   b. candidate
   c. citizen
   d. judge

5 a. alien
   b. woman
   c. citizen
   d. candidate

6 a. Africa
   b. the United States
   c. Hawaii
   d. Europe

What Does It Mean?

VOCABULARY

Read each sentence. Think about the underlined word. Write what the word probably means using the context clues in the sentence.

1 She <u>assumed</u> that the movie would be over soon, since the two main characters were again friends.

assumed _____

2 After a jolt of pain, he began <u>gasping</u> as the air was forced from his lungs.

gasping _____

3 She still had <u>misgivings</u> about whether or not she had made the right decision.

misgivings _____

4 The car swerved <u>erratically</u> as if it were out of the control of the driver.

erratically _____

5 If she peeked out the corner of the window of her bedroom, she could catch a <u>glimpse</u> of the ocean.

glimpse _____

6 There was an <u>urgency</u> in his voice as he made the announcement. It sent panic through the minds of many.

urgency _____

7 The directions were too <u>vague</u>, so the visitors were quickly lost in the city.

vague _____

8 She <u>derived</u> little satisfaction from the knowledge that they were only half way there.

derived _____

Reading Skills • 5-6 © 2004 Creative Teaching Press

Sentence Sense

VOCABULARY

Circle the word that correctly completes each sentence.

1 We had to fasten our seatbelts as the plane made its final (decent, descent).

2 He was (confident, confidant) that he was going to win the race.

3 I had (all ready, already) finished all my homework.

4 He made a (conscience, conscious) effort to stop laughing.

5 One (affect, effect) of rising prices is that people begin to buy less.

6 When they moved to Florida, they had to (adopt, adapt) to the warm weather.

7 Our city is trying to (eliminate, illuminate) pollution.

8 Everyone was invited to the party (accept, except) Kevin.

9 Betty receives many (complements, compliments) on her cooking.

10 The criminal (eluded, alluded) the police by hiding in an abandoned building.

11 The dog ran (thorough, through) the tunnel.

12 The camel walked throughout the arid (dessert, desert).

13 During rush hour, traffic was (stationery, stationary) for miles.

14 Mom asked her to (lay, lie) the plates on the table.

15 Jimmy has a newspaper (rout, route).

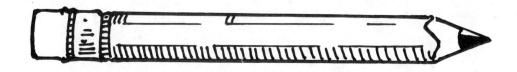

You Be the Dictionary

VOCABULARY

One of the hardest things to do with vocabulary is to define a word without using the word in the definition. Write the definition of each word without using the word or any form of it.

1. hamper_____

2. umbrella_____

3. ruler_____

4. envelope_____

5. mirror_____

6. stapler_____

7. heart_____

8. bird_____

9. ladder_____

10. flashlight_____

11. gavel_____

12. treadmill_____

13. map_____

14. advertisement_____

15. lotion_____

Reading Skills • 5-6 © 2004 Creative Teaching Press

Prefix Match-Up

VOCABULARY

The prefix **dis-** means "away from, opposite or absence of."
The prefix **mis-** means "wrong or wrongly, bad or badly."
The prefix **un-** means "not or the opposite of."

Match the definitions in Column B with the words beginning with the prefixes **dis-**, **mis-**, and **un-** in Column A. Write the letter on the line.

Column A

____ **1** unoccupied

____ **2** disgrace

____ **3** misleading

____ **4** undisturbed

____ **5** disapprove

____ **6** undecided

____ **7** mistreat

____ **8** disregard

____ **9** mispronounce

____ **10** unpopular

____ **11** dismiss

____ **12** misfortune

Column B

a. to treat badly

b. not liked or accepted

c. the loss of honor or respect

d. bad luck

e. causing a mistake or wrong idea

f. not bothered

g. not lived in

h. not having one's mind made up

i. to say a word or sound incorrectly

j to send away

k. to have a feeling against

l. to pay no attention to

Name _____   Date _____

Personal Opinion Questions
Question Comprehension

Answer each question and justify your answer. Hints: Begin your answer with a "yes" or a "no." Restate the vocabulary from the question in your complete answer. Answer in a complete sentence, citing a specific example or justification. Reread the question to make sure you fully answered it.

Example: Should children be paid an allowance?
Answer: Yes, children should be paid an allowance if they do chores around the house such as taking out the trash and making their bed.

1 Should fifth and sixth graders be allowed to stay at home alone?

_____

_____

2 Should every state have a helmet law requiring children and adults to wear helmets while riding bikes, motorcycles, and skateboards?

_____

_____

3 Should commercials for toys, sugary cereal, and candy be shown mostly on Saturday mornings?

_____

_____

4 Should school buses have seat belts like most other vehicles?

_____

_____

5 Should it be a state law to recycle all plastics, paper, and glass products?

_____

_____

6 Should children be allowed to watch television during the week?

_____

_____

7 Should teachers earn more money per year?

_____

_____

Reading Skills • 5-6 © 2004 Creative Teaching Press

Are You Serious?

QUESTION COMPREHENSION

Literal question—someone expects an answer.
   Example: Would you like to try my brownies?
Rhetorical question— someone is "making conversation" but doesn't expect an answer. This sounds like a question but the speaker doesn't expect you to say anything.
   Example: Can you believe I made these brownies myself?

Read each question. Decide if it is **literal** or **rhetorical**. Circle the type of question it is.

1. What did you have for breakfast this morning?   literal   rhetorical

2. Can you believe we have so much homework?   literal   rhetorical

3. Are you going to the movies on Saturday night?   literal   rhetorical

4. Are you nuts?   literal   rhetorical

5. She can't be serious?   literal   rhetorical

6. What are you reading?   literal   rhetorical

7. Can you imagine how silly I felt?   literal   rhetorical

8. What in the world was I thinking?   literal   rhetorical

9. May I borrow some tape, please?   literal   rhetorical

10. Which way do I turn at the next stop sign?   literal   rhetorical

11. Do you think money grows on trees?   literal   rhetorical

12. What did you get at the store?   literal   rhetorical

13. How many slices are in that pizza?   literal   rhetorical

14. Do you seriously expect me to believe that?   literal   rhetorical

15. How am I ever going to get all of this done on time?   literal   rhetorical

Name _____ Date _____

Always, Sometimes, Never
QUESTION COMPREHENSION

Some statements have a degree of truth to them. Read each statement and decide whether it is always true, sometimes true, or never true. Circle your choice.

1. A healthy dog has four legs.   always   sometimes   never

2. Worms emerge from cocoons.   always   sometimes   never

3. Birds live in nests.   always   sometimes   never

4. Strawberries grow on trees.   always   sometimes   never

5. Money should be saved.   always   sometimes   never

6. Students enjoy homework.   always   sometimes   never

7. Justice is fairly served.   always   sometimes   never

8. The President of the United States is elected every four years.   always   sometimes   never

9. Batteries can be recharged.   always   sometimes   never

10. The Statue of Liberty carries a torch.   always   sometimes   never

11. The post office is closed on national holidays.   always   sometimes   never

12. People work to earn money.   always   sometimes   never

13. Teachers are women.   always   sometimes   never

14. United States presidents are men.   always   sometimes   never

15. School starts in September.   always   sometimes   never

16. The planet Earth revolves around the sun.   always   sometimes   never

17. Real estate values go up every year.   always   sometimes   never

18. Rabbits live in groups in the wild.   always   sometimes   never

Reading Skills • 5-6 © 2004 Creative Teaching Press

Name _____   Date _____

You're the Teacher

QUESTION COMPREHENSION

Many teachers create questions to check for understanding. This time, you get to be the teacher. Read the passage. Then write 5 separate questions to ask *Who? What? When? Where? Why?* and *How?*

   Across America, there are more than 200 children's museums that are visited by children and adults alike. One fascinating museum is called the Adventure Children's Museum in Columbia, South Carolina. One highlight of this museum is the forty-foot-tall human body named Eddie. Kids can climb around inside of him and even stomp on his brain! In the last ten years, museum attendance has increased four times over to an average of 30 million visitors a year. Why do so many families and schools visit children's museums across the United States? Perhaps it's the emphasis on making learning fun! Some offer exhibit areas such as virtual reality orchestras, hands-on fossil exploration, and interactive robotic displays. Others offer art studios and science labs! Whether you're interested in the past, present, or the future, there's a museum just waiting for you to visit. In fact, there are more than 80 children's museums preparing to open soon.

Who?_____

What? _____

When? _____

Where? _____

Why? _____

How?_____

Name _____ Date _____

You're the Teacher Again

QUESTION COMPREHENSION

Many teachers create questions to check for understanding. This time, you get to be the teacher. Read the passage. Then write 5 separate questions to ask *Who? What? When? Where? Why?* and *How?*

Rabbits are social mammals that live in groups. They are prey for many animals, so they are always alert to their environment. This also explains why they have eyes on the sides of their skulls. All animals that have this eye placement are considered prey on the food chain. They must always watch their surroundings. Animals that have eyes placed at the front of their skulls are predators who are constantly on the hunt. Rabbits primarily eat grasses and vegetables; therefore, they are herbivores. As herbivores, they have flat teeth for grinding their food. On the contrary, their predators have sharp teeth since they are carnivores (meat eaters). Rabbits are particularly good at observing their environment at the same time as grazing on the natural foods around them. Living in groups helps these social animals, since they warn each other with foot stomps on the ground when they sense danger. Immediately, the others in the group will run to shelter. Fortunately for the rabbits, most predators cannot get into their burrows, so they safely huddle together until the predators depart.

Who?_____

What? _____

When? _____

Where? _____

Why? _____

How?_____

Reading Skills • 5-6 © 2004 Creative Teaching Press

Name _____ Date _____

Marshmallow Cereal Bars

INTERPRETING WRITTEN DIRECTIONS

Interpreting written directions is a life skill based on comprehension of functional print (text that helps you function in society). The language is different since most sentences are direct with few adjectives or flowery language.

Read the recipe. Then answer the questions.

Microwave a ¼ cup of butter in a glass mixing bowl on HIGH for 45–60 seconds or until it melts. Stir in one package of marshmallows along with a ¼ cup of peanut butter. Microwave on HIGH for 1 to 2 minutes until it melts. Stir the mixture until smooth. Add 6 cups of cereal and 2 cups of peanuts. Stir thoroughly. Press the mixture into a buttered 12 x 8 in. baking dish with the back of a large wooden spoon. Place in the refrigerator for 30 minutes to solidify. Cut bars. Recipe makes a dozen marshmallow cereal bars.

1 What setting will you use on your microwave? _____

2 What gets mixed together with the cereal?_____

3 How do you know when the butter has been in the microwave long enough?_____

4 What size baking dish do you need? _____

5 List all of the ingredients you need for this recipe._____

_____

6 What should you do before you cut apart the bars? _____

7 How much peanut butter do you need?_____

8 If you were making this for your class, would there be enough bars? Why or why not?

_____

_____

Reading Skills • 5–6 © 2004 Creative Teaching Press

Name _____   Date _____

Handy Dandy Card Holder

INTERPRETING WRITTEN DIRECTIONS

Read the directions for making a Handy Dandy Card Holder. Then answer the questions in complete sentences.

Get two lids from small, clear plastic margarine tubs. Poke a hole in the center of each lid. Get a metal brad (fastener). Put the two plastic lids together with the grooves on the outside facing each other. Place the metal brad through the two lids until they are connected. Decorate the outside with permanent markers or stickers. Slip your playing cards in between the two lids of your card holder.

1 List all of the materials you need to make the card holder.

_____

2 Why do you think the plastic lids need to be clear?

_____

3 Why do you think the outside should be decorated with permanent markers versus washable markers?

_____

4 What would happen if the lids were different sizes?

_____

5 Why do you think it makes a difference which direction the lids are facing?

_____

Draw a picture of what you think the Handy Dandy Card Holder looks like.

Reading Skills • 5-6 © 2004 Creative Teaching Press

What's the Answer?

INTERPRETING WRITTEN DIRECTIONS

Follow the directions in order to find the answer to the question.

> **Which state is the fourth largest with the forty-fourth largest population?**
>
> Answer: _____

Cross out the state names that
- have an **s**
- end with an **o**
- have two words
- end with a consonant

- have an **r**
- do not have 3 syllables
- begin with a vowel
- do not have a **t**

Alabama	Indiana	Nebraska	South Carolina
Alaska	Iowa	Nevada	South Dakota
Arizona	Kansas	New Hampshire	Tennessee
Arkansas	Kentucky	New Jersey	Texas
California	Louisiana	New Mexico	Utah
Colorado	Maine	New York	Vermont
Connecticut	Maryland	North Carolina	Virginia
Delaware	Massachusetts	North Dakota	Washington
Florida	Michigan	Ohio	West Virginia
Georgia	Minnesota	Oklahoma	Wisconsin
Hawaii	Mississippi	Oregon	Wyoming
Idaho	Missouri	Pennsylvania	
Illinois	Montana	Rhode Island	

Name _____ Date _____

Hawaiian Pizza

Interpreting Written Directions

Read the recipe and answer the questions.

Preheat the broiler. Cut a long loaf of French bread in half lengthwise. Spread 1½ cups of pizza sauce over both sides of the bread. Cut apart 4 ounces of Canadian bacon. Put the bacon on top of the sauce. Cut apart 1 small bell pepper. Put the pieces on the bacon. Open 1 can of pineapple. Put the pieces on top of the bell peppers and ham. Shred 2 cups of mozzarella cheese. Sprinkle the cheese on top of the other toppings. Broil for about 10 minutes or until the cheese melts. Let cool. Slice each in half. Servings—4

1 List all of the ingredients you will need to make the Hawaiian Pizza._____

_____

2 What do you do first? _____

3 What toppings are there? _____

4 What is the order of the toppings from bottom to top? _____

_____

5 Why do you think the recipe specifically asks for mozzarella cheese?

_____

6 How many ounces of bacon do you need? _____

7 Why do you think you need to cut the bell pepper? _____

8 What do you do last? _____

Reading Skills • 5-6 © 2004 Creative Teaching Press

Four in Four

CATEGORIZATION

Categorization is the method of grouping things based on similarities. In order to create a category and put details within it, one must be able to analyze, reason, and apply vocabulary knowledge.

Sort each group of words into four categories. Label the categories.

lasagna lobster		
pear plum		
tuna spaghetti		
cranberry sea urchin		
euro pizza		
marlin dollar		
orange yen		
pound bruschetta		

Erie South America		
Portugal Michigan		
Asia Superior		
Africa Netherlands		
Roosevelt Bush		
Spain Europe		
Ontario Canada		
Carter Lincoln		
Huron		

music monitor		
aquamarine sky		
science engine		
keyboard slate		
turquoise history		
caboose rail		
math disk drive		
mouse		
car		

Elimination

CATEGORIZATION

Categorization is the method of grouping things based on similarities. In order to create a category and put details within it, one must be able to analyze, reason, and apply vocabulary knowledge. When something does not belong in a category with other items, then it is eliminated.

Read each set of items. Cross out the one that does not belong in the same category as the rest. Explain why it does not belong.

1 baseball   tennis   throw   football

_____

2 bedroom   building   dining room   kitchen

_____

3 wet   coffee   water   tea

_____

4 Bush   Washington   Adams   Perot

_____

5 Erikson   Magellan   Hudson   Aldrich

_____

6 license   subscription   prescription   menu

_____

7 balloon   bicycle   raft   ball

_____

8 concrete   fur   steel   diamond

_____

9 frustrated   happy   melancholy   smile

_____

Reading Skills • 5-6 © 2004 Creative Teaching Press

A Full House

CATEGORIZATION

Look at the category written on the roof of each house. Write four words that belong in the house.

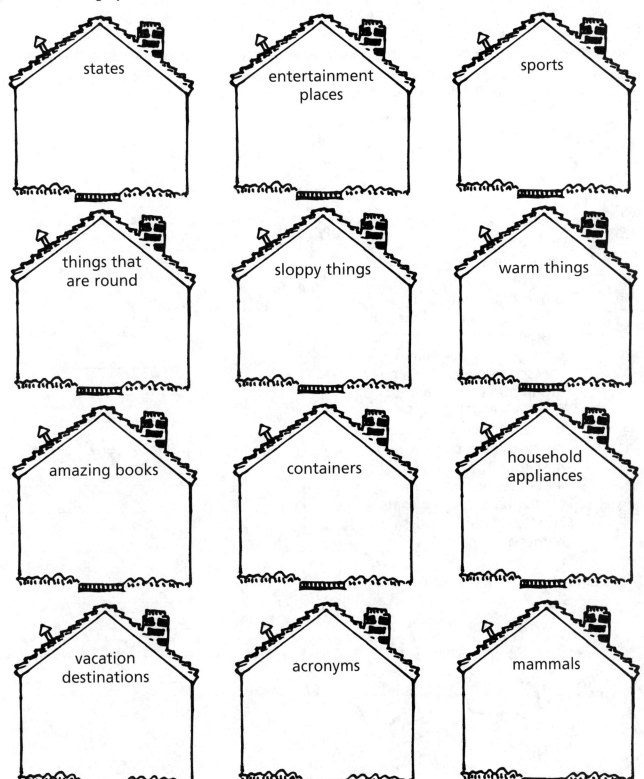

states

entertainment places

sports

things that are round

sloppy things

warm things

amazing books

containers

household appliances

vacation destinations

acronyms

mammals

The Outline

CATEGORIZATION

Categorization is the method of grouping things based on similarities. When you make an outline, you are using categorization.

Read the paragraph. Then fill in the missing parts of the outline. The categories are the main ideas (roman numerals). The details are the examples (the letters).

In order to grow up healthy and strong, it is important for all children to eat a balanced diet. The Food Pyramid is one organizational tool, although other diets consist of the same basic nutritional groups. The dairy group includes milk, cheese, and yogurt. The meat group consists of poultry, beef, fish, and dried beans. The breads and cereals group includes pasta, tortillas, and macaroni. The vegetable group includes broccoli, asparagus, carrots, and brussel sprouts. The fruit group includes raspberries and pears.

A Balanced Diet

I. Dairy Group

    A. _____

    B. _____

    C. _____

II. Meat Group

    A. _____

    B. _____

    C. _____

    D. _____

III. Breads and Cereals

    A. _____

    B. _____

    C. _____

IV. Vegetable Group

    A. _____

    B. _____

    C. _____

    D. _____

V. Fruit Group

    A. _____

    B. _____

Reading Skills • 5-6 © 2004 Creative Teaching Press

Name _____ Date _____

What Category?

CATEGORIZATION

Classifying is giving a name to a group of things in order to describe what the items have in common. Classifying can help you select and organize details.

Read each group of words. Decide what the words have in common. Then write a word or phrase that names or labels the list.

1. _____ chess   checkers   dominoes   cards

2. _____ poodle   dalmation   labrador   terrier

3. _____ polka   hula   ballet   tango

4. _____ Picasso   Van Gogh   Mondrian   Warhol

5. _____ rose   petunia   daisy   geranium

6. _____ basketball   baseball   soccer   tennis

7. _____ trumpet   tuba   saxophone   trombone

8. _____ pants   shirt   sweater   skirt

9. _____ magazine   newspaper   letter   textbook

10. _____ Washington   Kennedy   Ford   Adams

11. _____ thermometer   scale   ruler   speedometer

12. _____ Bach   Beethoven   Handel   Tchaikovsky

Reading Skills • 5-6 © 2004 Creative Teaching Press

The Big Idea

MAIN IDEA

The **main idea** is the title of a category of details. By understanding that you group words into categories, you understand that you group details into a main idea. This is the first step to understanding the main idea of anything you read.

Read each set of details. Write the main idea in the middle of the TV.

monitor · keyboard · mouse · memory	penny · quarter · nickel · dime	Bush · Lincoln · Clinton · Washington
Huron · Ontario · Erie · Superior	west · north · east · south	broccoli · cauliflower · carrots · asparagus
tennis · basketball · track · water polo	doctor · plumber · teacher · accountant	water · juice · coffee · soda
French · German · Latin · Dutch	snake · crocodile · lizard · alligator	algebra · exponents · division · percentages
clear · foggy · rainy · overcast	vanilla · raspberry · mint · chocolate	Asia · Africa · Europe · Australia

Reading Skills • 5–6 © 2004 Creative Teaching Press

How Supportive Are You?

MAIN IDEA

> When writing a story or reading a book, the ideas start with a topic sentence. This is usually the main idea. Next there should be sentences that provide details that support the main idea.

Read each main idea that could be developed into a paragraph. Write a checkmark on the line if the sentence listed below the main idea would be a good supporting detail to include in the paragraph. Choose only the details that directly relate to the main idea.

1 **Main idea:** how homemade paper is made
   a. _____ Paper comes from trees.
   b. _____ The blender turns the paper into pulp.
   c. _____ Homemade paper is used to make greeting cards.
   d. _____ Shredded paper is placed into a blender with water.
   e. _____ You can sell homemade paper for at least $1.00 a sheet.
   f. _____ You need to rip used construction paper or newspaper into thin strips.

2 **Main idea:** safety rules for the road
   a. _____ You should never plug too many things into one outlet.
   b. _____ You should always wear a helmet while on a bike.
   c. _____ Don't use an electrical appliance near water.
   d. _____ Don't ride in a car without putting on your seatbelt first.
   e. _____ Drivers shouldn't eat and talk on their cell phones while driving.
   f. _____ Don't open the door to strangers.

3 **Main idea:** owl pellets hold bones
   a. _____ When dissecting an owl pellet, you'll find ribs and skulls.
   b. _____ Owls prey upon mice, moles, and other small rodents.
   c. _____ If you're careful, you can remove the hair and discover tiny shoulder blades.
   d. _____ Owls are nocturnal and hunt for their prey at night.
   e. _____ The bones can be reconstructed and analyzed to determine what the owl ate for dinner.

4 **Main idea:** Goldilocks had bad manners
   a. _____ She ran away from the bears' home.
   b. _____ She ate someone's food without asking.
   c. _____ She slept in someone's bed without permission.
   d. _____ She broke someone's chair and didn't offer to pay for it.
   e. _____ She was out in the forest all alone.

Prove It!

MAIN IDEA

After reading any paragraph, you should have the main idea of what the author wanted to convey. When reading a novel, long book, or textbook, these main ideas are the most important for you to remember.

Read each paragraph. Write the main idea at the top. Underline three details in the paragraph that support your main idea.

Main Idea: _____
_____

    The largest invertebrate group contains all the arthropods. Did you know that scientists have found about nine million different species of arthropods in our world? Arthropods have a hard exoskeleton and jointed legs. There are five classes, or categories, of arthropods: insects, crustaceans, arachnids, centipedes, and millipedes. Most of the animals that we call "bugs" are really arthropods. One way to tell them apart is by the number of legs they have. Crustaceans, like crabs and shrimp, have ten legs. Arachnids, which include spiders, ticks, and scorpions, have eight legs. Their bodies are made of sections.

Main Idea: _____
_____

    The Great Depression began in 1929. It was the worst and longest period of unemployment in our history. At one time, one-fourth of the working people did not have jobs. It was also the worst and longest period of slow business growth. Nobody could afford to buy things and businesses failed.

Reading Skills • 5-6 © 2004 Creative Teaching Press

Main Idea and Details

MAIN IDEA

Read the paragraph. Decide what the main idea is and find three supporting details.

Due to the booming technology industry, there are many new computer-related jobs being created every day. This is good news for those people who have a keen interest in computer technology. The jobs currently available include web page designers, online auction resellers, computer technicians, software developers, and computer engineers. Jobs of the future will involve the health care sector even more. Computer engineers are developing different ways that computers can help the disabled and stroke victims as well as doctors and nurses. Someday, hospitals could be completely run by computers and robots. How would you feel about having a robot for a doctor? As the computer age develops, what once seemed impossible is now indeed possible. Who knows what lies ahead!

Main Idea: _____

Supporting Details:

_____

_____

_____

_____

_____

_____

Name _____ Date _____

Paired Up

PREDICTING

A **prediction** is a combination of your prior knowledge plus what you read plus your conclusion about what was read. What comes to your mind while you are reading plays a big part in the type of predictions that you make.

Read each word. Write down the first word that pops into your head. This is your immediate background knowledge. This is what comes into play when you make predictions. Next, find someone else to complete the activity. Say each word and write down the first word the person says. Do you think alike?

Word Associations	Me	Someone Else
1. boys and		
2. bacon and		
3. cat and		
4. paper and		
5. give and		
6. sickness and		
7. salt and		
8. stop and		
9. fork and		
10. good and		
11. questions and		
12. trial and		
13. brother and		
14. old and		
15. milk and		
16. dollars and		
17. peanuts and		
18. stars and		
19. prince and		
20. tortoise and		
21. thick and		
22. richer or		
23. sticks and		
24. cheese and		
25. macaroni and		

Reading Skills • 5–6 © 2004 Creative Teaching Press

Get Logical!

PREDICTING

Read each situation. Using logic, decide what will most likely happen next based on the facts and your background knowledge. Write your predictions. Your predictions must be based on ALL of the facts, not just some of them.

1 Danielle and Ellie wanted to watch their favorite cartoons.
Their dad wanted to watch a movie that was on at the same time.
They only have one television in their house.

Prediction: _____

2 Ian has a stomachache.
Ian always says he's feeling sick, although it's usually not true.
School starts in a half hour.

Prediction: _____

3 On his way home from work, Tom's car had a flat tire.
Tom didn't have the tools he needed to change the tire himself.
Tom was on the freeway when it happened.

Prediction: _____

4 Grandma baked her infamous chocolate chip cookies.
They were piping hot on the counter.
Her three grandchildren walked in from school.

Prediction: _____

5 The cable always goes out in a storm.
The weatherman is predicting three inches of rain.
The sky is gray and the air is cold.

Prediction: _____

Name _____ Date _____

Predictions Aren't Perfect

PREDICTING

Read each situation. Draw a conclusion from what you read. Write a prediction based on your prior knowledge of the situation plus your reading plus your conclusion. Cover up the page so you see only one problem at a time. Change your predictions as you read each additional sentence.

1 Cindi went to the hospital.

Conclusion:_____

Prediction: _____

2 Cindi put on her uniform and reported to the nurses' station.

Conclusion:_____

Revised Prediction: _____

3 Cindi was very tired, but she knew she had an important job to do.

Conclusion:_____

Prediction: _____

4 The phone call told her that her patient, Mrs. Smith, was ready to deliver.

Conclusion:_____

Prediction: _____

5 Luckily, Cindi made it into the labor and delivery room just in the knick of time.

Conclusion:_____

Prediction: _____

6 The delivery was a success, and the baby was named after her.

Conclusion:_____

Prediction: _____

7 Cindi Smith was very pleased with her work that night as were her patients.

Conclusion:_____

Prediction: _____

8 Cindi knew it would be a few years before she got to experience that again.

Conclusion:_____

Prediction: _____

Reading Skills • 5-6 © 2004 Creative Teaching Press

Name _____ Date _____

Television Titles

Predicting

Read each title. Predict what each television show will be about.

1   Our Wild World   Prediction: _____
_____

2   Travelin' Tanya   Prediction: _____
_____

3   Concert for Kids   Prediction: _____
_____

4   Build 'Em Up!   Prediction: _____
_____

5  Water Racing   Prediction: _____
_____

6   Airflight: A History   Prediction: _____
_____

7  A Farmer's Life   Prediction: _____
_____

8 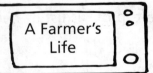 Football Frenzy   Prediction: _____
_____

Reading Skills • 5-6 © 2004 Creative Teaching Press

Get to Know the Character

CHARACTERIZATION

Read the story. Then read each statement about the characters. Circle **True** or **False**.

Upon arriving at school one day, Pat realized that he had forgotten to do his homework. Since the completion of homework was part of his grade, he knew he had to turn it in. It was too late to actually do it correctly. He had to make a quick decision. Just then, his friend Claire walked by. He asked Claire if he could quickly copy her homework so his grade wouldn't go down. She gave him a stern look, but she quickly gave in when he offered to pay her back somehow. Knowing Claire always got good grades made Pat's decision even easier. This way he would not only turn in his homework, but get a good grade at the same time. While he was quickly copying down the answers, Claire's friend Sydney walked by. She asked what was going on since she was suspicious of what she saw. Claire explained the situation to Sydney. Sydney quickly said that she had to hurry to her class because she didn't want to be late. They agreed to meet in the quad at lunchtime since they didn't have any classes together. Meanwhile, Pat finished copying the homework assignment. Pat and Claire walked to class. They arrived just as the bell began to ring. Imagine Pat's shock, when his teacher walked right over to his table and ripped his homework paper in half!

True   False   **1**   At first, Claire was annoyed with Pat's request.

True   False   **2**   Pat is usually honest.

True   False   **3**   Claire was gullible and easily talked into doing something wrong.

True   False   **4**   Sydney showed the strongest positive character traits in the story.

True   False   **5**   Sydney values fairness and discipline.

True   False   **6**   Pat puts respect and consideration at the top of his list of behaviors.

True   False   **7**   Claire was an honest student.

True   False   **8**   Sydney was an honest student.

True   False   **9**   Pat is probably trustworthy.

True   False   **10**   Claire has motivation and self-discipline.

Reading Skills • 5-6 © 2004 Creative Teaching Press

Name _____ Date _____

Casting Call

CHARACTERIZATION

Read the list of actors and actresses who arrived at a casting call to try out for parts in the upcoming movie titled *Strange Days in Yountville*. Then match each role to the person who will probably be assigned to play it. (Clue: The stage names relate to the characters exactly.)

_____ 1 Dory Darefisher

_____ 2 Bravado Bernardo

_____ 3 Frannie Fearladen

_____ 4 Lori Leaderlorn

_____ 5 Connie Catastrophe

_____ 6 Susan Smart

_____ 7 John Jokester

_____ 8 Vin Villaintino

_____ 9 Tuck Trustmason

_____ 10 Hildy Honesty

_____ 11 Carla Carealot

_____ 12 Benny Boastman

_____ 13 Ellie Efficiency

_____ 14 Hope Harrington

_____ 15 Joy Jessington

a. loves to read while lying in the sun; she always tells the truth

b. will try anything; fearless; loves to be dared

c. moves quickly; gets her work done on time; uses her time wisely

d. laughs often; has a positive attitude; happy about her life

e. people believe him; people confide in him; he keeps secrets well

f. is not afraid of new situations; will try something although a bit scared

g. intelligent; planner; enrolled in grad school

h. comedian; tries to make all other characters laugh; always goofing around

i. the bad character in the movie; the character others are scared of

j. planner; boss of the business; tells others what to do in a nice manner

k. scared of everything and everyone; won't go outside due to extreme fears

l. brags all the time; has few friends; annoys most other characters around him

m. looks on the bright side; doesn't give up; she's constantly thinking things will get better

n. always in a mess; disasters follow her; disorganized

o. loving character; takes care of everyone else; gives of herself without expecting in return

Name _____ Date _____

A Feel for the Character

CHARACTERIZATION

Read each emotion in the word box. Then read each sentence and write the emotion that best describes how the character is feeling.

happiness	frustration	disgust	despair	worry
excitement	anger	nervousness	hope	fear

_____ Pam believed her lost puppy would return home soon.

_____ Molly couldn't wait another minute. Her mom was coming off the airplane any minute!

_____ Frank kept checking his watch. He didn't want to be late for the big meeting.

_____ Jasmine couldn't believe what she was seeing. That man was picking his nose!

_____ Ben gave up. He knew he wouldn't get out of the mess. There was no way to avoid it.

_____ The line was so long at the restaurant that the guests were beginning to complain.

_____ Being afraid of heights, Lennie was about to cry while going up on the roller coaster.

_____ Since she always had a smile on her face, everyone enjoyed being with Sarah.

_____ As the helicopter took off, the feeling in her stomach went away and she began to relax.

_____ When Yoko yelled her face turned bright red.

Reading Skills • 5-6 © 2004 Creative Teaching Press

Name _____ Date _____

Traits on Plates

CHARACTERIZATION

Read each license plate. Write two character traits that might describe the driver who chose the plates.

1  in2risk

_____   _____

2 bravboy

_____   _____

3  imsmart

_____   _____

4  icuhlp2

_____   _____

5  nvrgvup

_____   _____

6  urkind2

_____   _____

7  imonist

_____   _____

8  neverl8

_____   _____

9  apolit1

_____   _____

10 icare4u

_____   _____

Matching Settings

SETTING

Read each description of a setting. Match it to the location the author is describing.

_____ **a.** stormy day   _____ **f.** swimming pool

_____ **b.** beach in the summer   _____ **g.** desert

_____ **c.** garden   _____ **h.** rain forest

_____ **d.** crowded city   _____ **i.** laboratory

_____ **e.** ake   _____ **j.** library

1 Many people were relaxing while doing research or simply reading. People were walking in and out the front door throughout the day, but the room always remained quiet.

2 The splashing was a sign of the fun every child was having on the beautiful day. The children were trying not to splash the adults who were lounging on rafts sunbathing. The smell of chlorine indicated that the water was recently cleaned.

3 People were rushing past each other on their way to work. It was amazing how many people were dressed up in business suits carrying briefcases and cups of coffee. Being there on a busy Monday was not a smart thing for a traveler to do.

4 The boat seemed to glide through the water. At daybreak, there were only a few waterskiiers, so Carlos was able to drive his boat even faster! Within hours, there would be almost a hundred boats and jet skis on the glassy water creating waves, which were difficult to ski on.

5 It was dark and gloomy outside and everything was wet so we played inside.

6 The hot sun and dry climate made Marcus even more thirsty than usual. As he was opening his canteen, he saw a rattlesnake emerge from its hole.

7 The test tubes and graduated cylinders were filled with solutions. The white room was clean, organized, and clutter free. This allowed the workers to conduct experiments without getting their solutions contaminated.

8 The ladybugs and butterflies were happy there. It was a peaceful environment. The kids picked fruits and vegetables and smelled the lovely flowers.

9 It was dark on the bottom layer, not much sunlight got to the area. In the next layer, there was a little more sunlight. Many animals like frogs, snakes, and jaguars lived there.

10 Everyone seemed to be wearing a bathing suit. Many children were building sand castles with shovels and buckets. People were walking along the water.

Reading Skills • 5-6 © 2004 Creative Teaching Press

Get in the Mood

Setting

> The **setting** tells about time and place. It is also used to help set the mood or tone of the story. The adjectives used to describe the setting help readers picture the events of the story.

Pretend you are an author. You are writing a book in which the character is traveling. Your character will encounter different events that will affect the mood of the story. What details would you include for each of the following situations?

Your character is going to encounter some happy events. Write three details that could be used to describe the setting that would make him or her happy.

1 _____

2 _____

3 _____

Your character is going to encounter some frightening events. Write three details that could be used to describe the setting that would make him or her scared.

1 _____

2 _____

3 _____

Your character is going to encounter some relaxing events. Write three details that could be used to describe the setting that would make him or her calm and relaxed.

1 _____

2 _____

3 _____

Your character is going to encounter some exciting events. Write three details that could be used to describe the setting that would make him or her extremely overjoyed.

1 _____

2 _____

3 _____

Name _____ Date _____

It's in the Details

SETTING

Read the mood the author wants to evoke. Write the best setting for this mood. Write the details that would be necessary for the setting to evoke these moods.

Mood	Setting	Vivid Details
suspense		
excitement		
fear		
nervousness		
joy		
worry		
anger		
sadness		

Reading Skills • 5–6 © 2004 Creative Teaching Press

Ready on the Set

SETTING

The director has the sets ready for his commercials. Read the description of each product that will be advertised. Choose the best backdrop for the set of the commercial.

1 The medicine helps kids feel better quickly. It reduces the fever and stops the coughing.
- ○ classroom
- ○ hospital
- ○ bedroom

2 The vitamins make kids healthy and happy. When they take their vitamins they have more energy.
- ○ classroom
- ○ playground
- ○ restaurant

3 The new scooter comes in many colors. It has handlebars that extend up to any height. The braking system is safe and easy. The scooter turns a full 360 degrees with the push of one button.
- ○ toy store
- ○ parking lot
- ○ street in front of house

4 The new CD player is the size of a child's hand. It has the thickness of three CD's. It can fit in the front zipper of a backpack. The price is cheap. The attached earphones fit into a flap on the back.
- ○ toy store
- ○ school
- ○ car driving somewhere

5 The new food chopper slices and dices tomatoes, potatoes, carrots, lettuce, and many other vegetables and fruit. Making salsa or coleslaw from start to finish takes only 45 seconds. Cleanup includes a simple rinse in the sink.
- ○ cafeteria
- ○ dining room
- ○ kitchen

6 The wheels attach to the bottom of sneakers to become roller blades. They fold three ways to become flat for easy storage.
- ○ night time
- ○ Saturday morning on the block
- ○ recess time at school

7 The new shutters come with a locking device that is child proof. They can't be opened while in the locked position.
- ○ a teenager's room
- ○ a child's room
- ○ a toddler's room

8 The new pants have three sets of zippers that can be removed so the long pants become short pants or shorts. They easily zip back together. The pieces that come off fit into pockets on the shorts.
- ○ library
- ○ toy store
- ○ bedroom

Name _____ Date _____

What's Next?

SEQUENCING

To put something into a sequence is to put it in order.
Example: December, May, March in sequence is March, May, December

Sequence each set of circumstances into the correct order so that it makes sense to someone else. Write the numbers 1–5 with 1 being what comes first in the sequence.

____ Light the barbecue grill.
____ Take the meat out of the freezer.
____ Eat the hamburgers.
____ Put the hamburgers on the grill.
____ Cook the hamburgers.

____ Turn on the microwave.
____ Open the can of soup.
____ Pour it into the bowl.
____ Get a bowl and a can of soup.
____ Eat the soup.

____ Get some towels and shampoo.
____ Put the dog into the tub or shower.
____ Rinse the shampoo off with water.
____ Dry off the dog.
____ Wash the dog with the shampoo.

____ Get on the airplane.
____ Show your identification and check your luggage.
____ Drive to the airport.
____ Go through the security checkpoint.
____ Wait to get on the plane.

____ Open the box of cake mix.
____ Find all of the ingredients to follow the recipe.
____ Mix the ingredients together in a bowl.
____ Bake in the oven at 300 degrees for 40 minutes.
____ Pour the cake mix into a cake pan.

Sequence Your Life

SEQUENCING

To put something into a sequence is to put it in order.
Example: wake up, shower, go to school, eat lunch

For each set of circumstances write the next four things that you do in the typical situation. Write each event in the sequential timeline below.

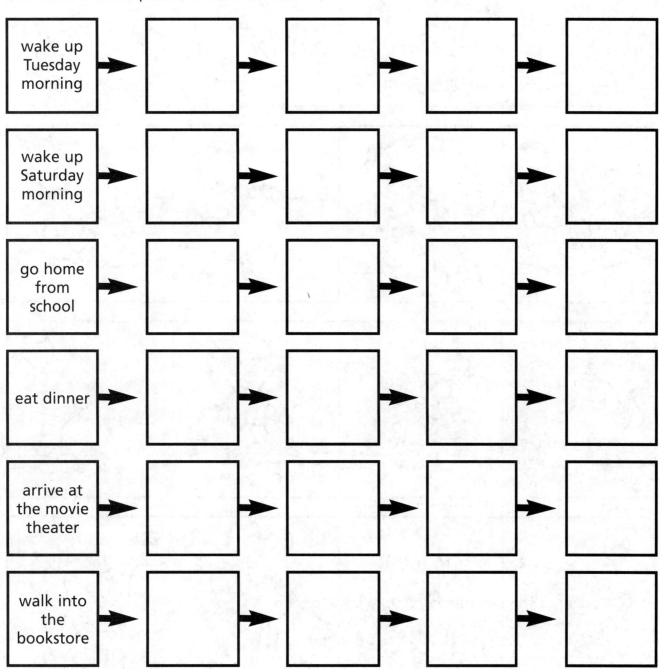

Reading Skills • 5–6 © 2004 Creative Teaching Press

Name _____ Date _____

Comics

SEQUENCING

Number each panel of the comic strip in correct sequential order.

Reading Skills • 5-6 © 2004 Creative Teaching Press

Name _____   Date _____

The Life of Bill Gates

Sequencing

Read the summary of the life of Bill Gates. Then fill in the graphic organizer with the important events that shaped his life in their correct sequence.

Bill Gates was born on October 28th, 1955 in Seattle, Washington. As a child, Bill was bored in school. He transferred to a private school that could challenge him more. It was there that he fell in love with computers. Within a week, he was better with computers than the computer teacher at his school! Bill was soon developing his own computer programs. He discovered a new place around the corner from his home that would allow him to use their computer for free in exchange for his computer expertise. This is when he met Paul Allen, who became his business partner for life. Together, they started a small company called Traf-O-Data. Their company included the software they developed which monitored the amount of traffic that went through a city. This was useful information for city developers, but it wasn't exactly a big success. However, the money was used for further learning by the two partners.

Bill Gates also developed a software program that arranged class schedules at his school. He conveniently ended up in all of the classes with the prettiest girls! He was greatly admired and considered to be one of the smartest students.

Bill graduated from high school and went on to Harvard University. Although he was still bored, it gave him the chance to develop more software programs for computers. His personal goal was to be a millionaire by the age of 30. After leaving Harvard to pursue business opportunities, he surpassed that goal by becoming a billionaire at the age of 31! In fact, this creator of Microsoft® was recently cited in a famous money magazine as the wealthiest man in the world and worth over $45 billion!

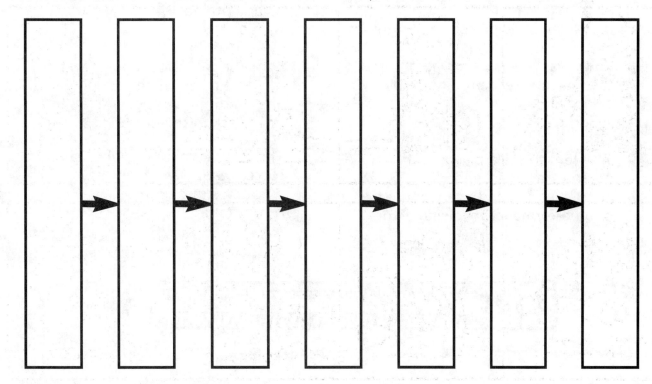

Name _____ Date _____

Which Meaning Makes Sense?

CONTEXT CLUES

> When good readers don't know what a word means, they look for **context clues**. Context clues are the words around the unknown words, the main idea of the paragraph, any images or illustrations, and parts of words.

Read each sentence and identify the multiple meaning word. Figure out which meaning is meant by the writer based on the context clues (words around the underlined word). Circle the letter next to the correct meaning.

1 Brenton asked, "Which <u>kind</u> of seasoning are you putting on the chicken tonight?"
   a. sweet
   b. type

2 Shiloh always <u>pants</u> when he walks around the park.
   a. an item of clothing worn on the legs
   b. breathes heavily

3 Farmer Guzman was trying to get his tractor back into his <u>shed</u>.
   a. to take something off
   b. a small building for storing things

4 Keith was trying to <u>light</u> the fire, but the matches kept burning out.
   a. not dark
   b. ignite

5 We went to see a <u>play</u> about a librarian last weekend.
   a. to have fun and enjoy oneself
   b. a performance involving actors

6 Will you please <u>check</u> to make sure your homework is already in your backpack?
   a. something that is filled out to pay for something
   b. to observe and verify

7 Are there any <u>rolls</u> left in that basket?
   a. to spin around and around
   b. round pieces of bread

8 She received a <u>fine</u> for sending her credit card payment in late.
   a. acceptable
   b. fee

9 Some people live along a <u>fault</u> line.
   a. to be responsible for doing something wrong
   b. a crack in the earth

10 The crowd went <u>wild</u> when the soccer team was victorious.
   a. crazy; out of control
   b. not tame

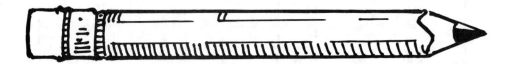

Reading Skills • 5-6 © 2004 Creative Teaching Press

Not So Tricky After All

CONTEXT CLUES

Read each sentence. Pay attention to the words around the underlined word, which may be unfamiliar to you. Use context clues to decide what the word most likely means. Write an explanation in the graphic organizer.

1. He gestured to his friend to join him at his table in the restaurant.

2. The stairs descended into a cavern that was colder than the area above it from which they began their journey.

3. Their path was barred by a swift-running river and high banks.

4. The more she contemplated what to do, the more she just couldn't decide.

5. She was upset when the horse she was accustomed to riding was given to another rider.

6. The naughty child was confined to his room until dinner.

7. The map was so complicated to read that she wondered if she'd ever get there.

8. Were the pirates the culprits? Were they responsible for the missing treasure chest?

Unfamiliar Word	Context Clue Meaning

Name _____   Date _____

Get to the Root of the Matter

Context Clues

Read the words. Look for parts of the words that you know the meaning of, including prefixes, suffixes, and roots. Complete the chart.

bi = two re = again co = with	de = down un = not ex = out	trans = across mit = send port = carry	sect = to cut ped = foot viv = life

Unfamiliar Word	Dissecting the Word	Meaning I Apply
trisect	tri = 3 sect = to cut	to cut into three sections
❶ transport		
❷ coexist		
❸ bisect		
❹ transmit		
❺ biped		
❻ revive		
❼ transect		
❽ export		
❾ remit		
❿ rejoin		

Reading Skills • 5-6 © 2004 Creative Teaching Press

Name _____ Date _____

Context Clues Crossword

Context Clues

Use context clues to fill in the missing word and complete the crossword puzzle.

enthusiasm	illusion	ecstatic	abundance
justice	context	predicament	velocity
optimistic	dispute	concoction	exhilarating

Across

2. She was _____ that she would win the race.
5. Her _____ over getting a good report card was obvious by her huge smile.
7. He thought he saw a leprechaun, but it was just an_____.
9. Whatever _____ his mother had cooking on the stove sure did smell terrible!
11. She was simply _____ when she won the trip to Europe.
13. It was an _____ feeling to be skiing for the first time!

Down

1. You are practicing the use of _____ clues to help reading comprehension.
3. The judge had to settle the _____ over who owned the land.
4. You expect _____ in a court of law.
6. What a _____ he was in! He just didn't know what to do!
8. The plane flew through the sky at an increasing _____.
10. She picked an _____ of avocados from her tree this year.

Name _____ Date _____

Context Clues

CONTEXT CLUES

You use **context clues** when you figure out the meaning of a word based on the words around it.
   Example: The team cheered triumphantly when they won the game. Triumphantly?
   It means "in an exciting way" since there was cheering and they won.

Read the sentences. Make a "meaning prediction" based on the context clues of each sentence. Then write the dictionary definition for each underlined word.

1 The mayor asked the people in his jurisdiction to vote in favor of a new bill requiring all dogs to be on leashes in his city.

2 You must justify your answer by providing examples from the story that prove what you think is going to happen can indeed be possible.

3 The boy tried to maneuver his bike around the cones, but they were too close together so he fell.

4 The final score of the game was so anticlimactic that most people simply got up and walked out without clapping or cheering at all.

5 The benefactor donated five thousand dollars to the needy charity. They were so grateful!

Vocabulary Word	My Meaning Prediction	Dictionary Definition
jurisdiction		
justify		
maneuver		
anticlimactic		
benefactor		

Reading Skills • 5-6 © 2004 Creative Teaching Press

Name _____ Date _____

Why Did It Happen?

CAUSE AND EFFECT

> **cause**—why something happened; answers the question "why?"
> **effect**—what happened; All causes have effects.
> For example, if you study hard for a test, then you may get an A. The studying was the cause that created the effect (the A). For every effect (result), there could be many different causes (reasons) why it happened.

Read the effects that are asking you why something occurred (the cause). Choose all causes that could have created the effect. Then add one more cause on your own.

1 A person goes to school to be a teacher. Why?
   a. He or she loves kids.
   b. He or she wants to be rich.
   c. He or she wants to help others.

Your cause for that person's decision:_____

2 A boy was stung by a bee. Why?
   a. He accidently stepped on it.
   b. He tried to catch it.
   c. He was in the mountains.

Your cause for the boy's bee sting:_____

3 The lady was given a treadmill for her birthday. Why?
   a. She was frail and just got out of the hospital.
   b. She will walk on it for two miles a day.
   c. She wanted to begin an exercise program.

Your cause for the birthday gift: _____

4 The fire department came to your school. Why?
   a. There was a false alarm.
   b. They were there to talk to the school about fire safety.
   c. They drove off after checking fire extinguishers.

Your cause for the visit: _____

5 Mr. Kominsky wrote a letter to the newspaper. Why?
   a. He was upset with something they printed in their paper.
   b. He wanted to thank them for their timely delivery every morning.
   c. He wanted to cancel his subscription.

Your cause for the letter: _____

Name _____ Date _____

What Happened?

CAUSE AND EFFECT

Read each event. It caused something to happen in each case. Try to unscramble the words to figure out what each effect was.

1 Chris was lazy. He didn't do his home-work and he didn't study at all. He took a history test on Wednesday and a math test on Friday.
Effect: dba   dsraeg

_____   _____

2 The Flynns live in a beach house right on the sand. A severe thunderstorm came through their town. If they had not prepared with the sandbags around the perimeter, what would the effect of the storm have been on their property?
Effect: ooddlfe

_____

3 Zach built a raft using wood that was less dense than water. He tried to put it in the water. What happened?
Effect: otdlfae

_____

4 A snowboarder went down the wrong run at the ski resort. The storm was rolling in. He was missing for 20 hours. What happened to him?
Effect: dseurce

_____

5 A volcano erupted in a highly popu-lated town. There were no injuries. How is this possible? What happened to the people?
Effect: daavueetc

_____

6 Linda loves to shop. She spends all of her money on her family. Her credit card bills are out of control. What does Linda have?
Effect: tebd

_____

7 Lindsay wanted to do a flip on the high beam in gymnastics. She'd never done it before and forgot to do her stretches. What happened?
Effect: erkbo   reh   mar

_____   _____   _____

8 Mario had severe asthma. While climbing a mountain, he had difficulty breathing. What did he do?
Effect: deus   sih   raihenl

_____   _____   _____

Reading Skills • 5-6 © 2004 Creative Teaching Press

What and Why?

CAUSE AND EFFECT

> **cause**—why something happened; answers the question "why?"
> **effect**—what happened

Read each sentence. Underline the cause (why) and circle the effect (what).

1. Debbie's mom broke her arm, so her dad got to do the cooking.

2. The dog broke off his leash, so he was running through the neighborhood.

3. Her favorite bagel shop was closed since it is remodeling and expanding.

4. He ended up in a computer store since his computer crashed.

5. Although she looked healthy, the daily hamburgers were giving her a high cholesterol level.

6. A famous author just became a billionaire because his books are adored the world over.

7. The movie let out early, because the electricity in the building went out.

8. She ran to the door to get the package because it was her birthday.

9. The rabbit nibbled on the dandelion greens since he was hungry.

10. The glue was dried out since the cap was left open all weekend.

11. A construction crew had to demolish the house since it was ruined in the hurricane.

12. She wanted to spend more time with her family, so she quit her job.

13. Because there were daily arguments over the gaming station, the boys' mother took it away.

14. Due to the increased level of air pollution, large trucks must pay higher license fees.

15. After eating five handfuls of jelly beans, the silly girl had a terrible stomachache.

Name _____ Date _____

The Good and the Bad of It All

CAUSE AND EFFECT

Read each cause. Write one positive and one negative effect or result from that cause.

You get a pet hamster.

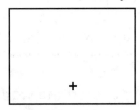 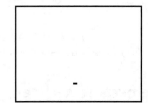

You stay up all night at the sleepover.

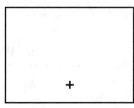 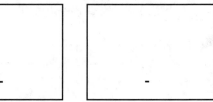

You eat a whole bag of cookies before you go to bed.

You have a dentist appointment.

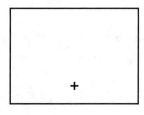 

You get a television for your bedroom.

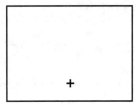 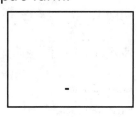

You are moving to a new school.

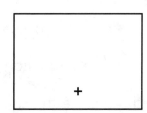 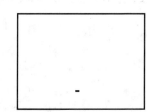

You are spending your vacation on your grandpa's farm.

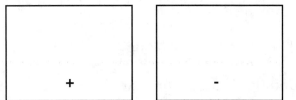

You get your hair cut a bit too short.

Reading Skills • 5-6 © 2004 Creative Teaching Press

Find the Cause or Effect

CAUSE AND EFFECT

Read each selection and complete the cause and effect boxes.

Adam planted some tomato seeds. He watered the seeds every day. He moved the pot to a window with lots of sunlight. He even added fertilizer to the soil. After a few weeks, a strong, healthy tomato plant grew.

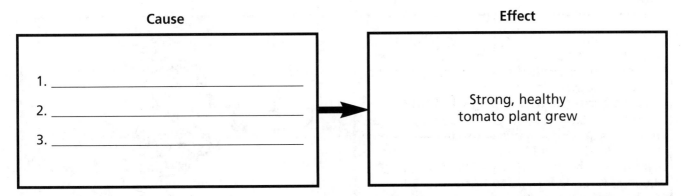

Cause

1. _____
2. _____
3. _____

Effect

Strong, healthy
tomato plant grew

Today was a sunny day. It was so bright that I needed my sunglasses. I wore shorts because of the heat.

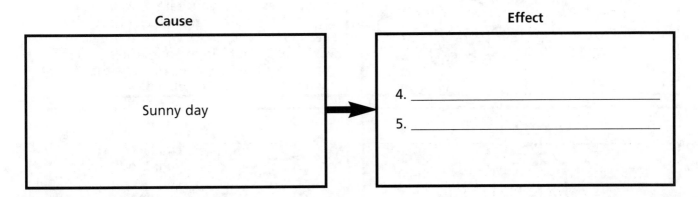

Cause

Sunny day

Effect

4. _____
5. _____

When Erin made the winning basket, a huge cheer went up from the crowd. This was the first time the team had won at home. Erin was named Most Valuable Player.

Cause

6. _____

Effect

7. _____
8. _____
9. _____

Name _____ Date _____

Alluring Advertisements

Fact and Opinion

A **fact** is something that can be proven. An **opinion** is how someone feels, thinks, or reacts to something. An opinion cannot be proven.

Look at the four advertisements. Underline all of the facts in the advertisements. Circle all of the opinions. Do the advertisements really tell the truth?

Another satisfied customer! We at Phillips Automotive know how much you care about buying a quality car. That's why we're #1 in customer satisfaction. We make the best cars and sell them at the best prices. You won't find a better car in any state! If you want more car for your money, then hustle on down to Phillips Automotive! We care about you. We care about the car you drive. We have over 3,000 cars ready for you to test drive. Hurry! Cars are moving fast! Just ask for me—Jeff Phillips. I'll give you what you deserve!

Hey kids! You know how much your family cares about your safety. Well, we do too! We've designed the all new Cool Cap! Everyone on your block wants to have one. Don't be left out. Go to your local sports shop and ask for the Cool Cap. You'll be the coolest kid on your block and you'll be safe!

Girl—Wow! That's the best tasting water in the world! It's hard to believe I'm taking my vitamins! Look Dad! I'm done. I can't wait to see what flavor I get tomorrow. Dad—I'm so proud of you! To think that we used to argue over vitamins. That's all over now thanks to Aguavites! There's no better way to take vitamins. That's why every parent in the world is trying new Aguavites. It gets everyone's day off to a great start.

It's the newest kitty craze! Every cat on your block will be at your door trying to get in when you fill your cat's bowl with Tasty Treats Cat Food. That's right, your cat will thank you every day for the delicious treat. Only you will know that it's not a treat—it's his food! There's not a cat who doesn't love Tasty Treats Cat Food. So . . . what are you waiting for? Run out and get some Tasty Treats Cat Food right away. Your cat will be healthier and happier. You'll know that you're giving your cat the best food on the market. Look for Tasty Treats Cat Food in the pet food aisle of your local pet store. Hurry! The stores are running out fast!

Reading Skills • 5-6 © 2004 Creative Teaching Press

Unscrambled Hints

FACT AND OPINION

The scrambled words are hints in sentences that you are reading _____ a fact. Unscramble the words. The first letter of each word is in bold.

m**s**see _____   yn**m**a _____

n**t**hik _____   rb**t**tee _____

ts**b**e _____   tw**r**so _____

l**l**a _____   lfwu**a** _____

vleee**b**i _____   or**e**eyevn _____

Read the sentences. Look for words that hint that you are reading opinions NOT facts. Circle the words that hinted the opinions.

1 Everyone loves the new Belle Chocolate Bar.

2 I think the main character is the protagonist.

3 Dogs are better than cats.

4 That's the worst roast beef I've ever eaten!

5 It seems like some people study harder than others.

6 You're the best reader in the class.

7 I believe that there's no better place to vacation than in the mountains.

8 Many people think that basketball is more exciting to watch than golf.

9 You're in an awful mess!

10 All children should eat their vegetables.

Name _____ Date _____

For Sale

FACT AND OPINION

Create an advertisement for a new product on the market from the list of choices below. List four facts and four opinions you can include in your ad. Finally, write your advertisement using your facts and opinions.

Choose your product to advertise:

movie	computer	shoes
cookies	pet product	beverage
restaurant	music CD	snack

List four facts about your product.

1 _____

2 _____

3 _____

4 _____

List four opinions you can make about the product.

1 _____

2 _____

3 _____

4 _____

Write the first draft of your advertisement using the facts and opinions you wrote above. Add enticing vocabulary to sell your product.

_____

_____

_____

_____

_____

_____

_____

_____

Reading Skills • 5-6 © 2004 Creative Teaching Press

The Flip Side

Fact and Opinion

Change the following opinions into statements that reflect facts.

Opinions	The Flip Side
❶ My teacher is the best in the world.	
❷ Our school should buy a parachute.	
❸ It seems like computers should cost less than televisions.	
❹ I believe that cauliflower tastes awful.	
❺ The high humidity seems to make me lazy.	
❻ The best thing to do in science class is an experiment.	
❼ Computers should be in every classroom in the United States.	

Change the following facts into statements that reflect opinions.

Facts	The Flip Side
❽ Birds migrate in the winter.	
❾ The sports arena was sold out.	
❿ It becomes more difficult to breathe as you go up in altitude.	
⓫ Regular coffee has caffeine.	
⓬ Solar energy can make some calculators work during the day.	
⓭ A ruler measures inches or centimeters.	
⓮ Penguins cannot fly, but ducks can.	

Reading Skills • 5–6 © 2004 Creative Teaching Press

Name _____ Date _____

Key Points

A **summary** tells the most important points of what is read. It omits details and focuses on main ideas. A summary should be short, and to the point. A summary tells only the key points of what was read.

Read each short paragraph. Write your summary in two sentences or less in the key next to the paragraph. Make sure that you only include the most important main ideas in your summary of key points.

Tom loves working on cars. Every weekend he spends most of his time trying to improve his vintage car so that it stays in top-notch condition. He's had the car for almost fifteen years. In that time, he's performed most of the repairs himself. In fact, he is so knowledgeable about cars that he's successfully fixed his brakes and flat tires and replaced the engine. His passion for the care and preservation of cars goes back to his childhood.

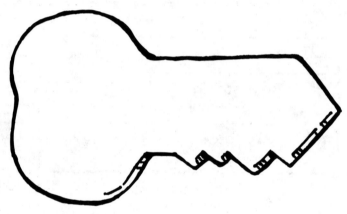

The pet caretaking business isn't financially rewarding, but it is fun. At least that's what Pauli discovered when she opened her Home Buddies Pet Service. She takes care of just about any domestic animal, including cats, birds, dogs, hamsters, lizards, and rabbits. When she realized how many people needed to work and couldn't take their pets on daily walks, she decided to open her business. Many of her clients also use her services when they travel out of town. She will even move into their house to care for the animals who get homesick! Her dedication makes her the best choice for people who love their pets.

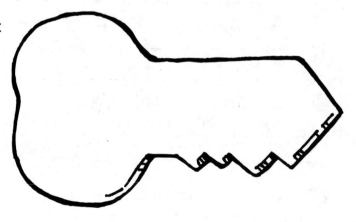

Reading Skills • 5-6 © 2004 Creative Teaching Press

Name _____ Date _____

Big Ideas of a Summary

SUMMARIZING

Below you will find the big ideas that remind you of what a summary should include and not include. However, these big ideas are all mixed up. Rearrange the words to write the reminders in the light bulbs that represent the "big ideas."

1
Summary written own your should in be words the.

2
Should information important the most presented be first.

3
Ideas and important main should only details be included.

_____   _____   _____
_____   _____   _____
_____   _____   _____

4
Most characters be the should named important.

5
Be vocabulary there directly should from the summary in the reading.

_____   _____
_____   _____
_____   _____

6
The complete should be summary but short.

7
Clear the summary should be.

8
Any summary there should not be in the your of opinions.

_____   _____   _____
_____   _____   _____
_____   _____   _____

Reading Skills • 5–6 © 2004 Creative Teaching Press

Comical Summaries

SUMMARIZING

Read each comic and then write a one- or two-sentence summary of what occurred. Remember to include only the most important ideas, name the characters, and mention only facts from the comic.

My summary

_____

_____

My summary

_____

_____

My summary

_____

_____

Reading Skills • 5–6 © 2004 Creative Teaching Press

Summarize Anything

SUMMARIZING

A **graphic organizer** can be used to summarize any book, novel, story, article, or ad. Read a newspaper or magazine article and fill in the information to practice summary writing. Use the checklist as a reminder of what to do when writing a summary.

Headline or Title: _____

Author: _____

Key characters or people included:

_____

_____

Vocabulary to include:

_____

_____

Main ideas:

_____

_____

_____

_____

_____

My summary:

_____

_____

_____

_____

_____

_____

_____

Summary checklist:
____The summary is written in my own words.
____The most important information was presented first.
____It includes only main ideas and important details.
____I named the most important characters/people.
____The summary includes vocabulary directly from the reading.
____The summary is short but complete.
____It is clear.
____My opinions are not in the summary.

Reading Skills • 5-6 © 2004 Creative Teaching Press

Plot Parts

PLOT

> The **plot** of a story is the series of events from the beginning to the end. The level of excitement or tragedy changes throughout the book based on the plot of the story.

Match each part of a plot to its definition.

_____ **1** events

_____ **2** resolution

_____ **3** introduction

_____ **4** conclusion

_____ **5** falling action

_____ **6** conflict

_____ **7** turning point

a. This part of the plot is how the conflict is solved.

b. This is the part of the story in which we meet the characters and begin to picture the setting.

c. This is where the story ends.

d. This is when we learn about the problems the characters must solve.

e. This is when the problems are solved and the story is getting ready to end.

f. This is the solution to a problem.

g. These are the twists, turns, and things that happen in the story.

Use six of the plot parts from above to label each part of this plot diagram.

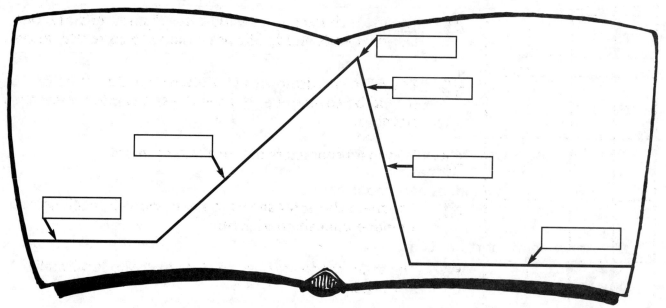

Conflicts

PLOT

> There are four major types of conflicts within the plot line of a story.
> **Person against person**—a character has a problem with at least one other character
> **Person against society**—a character has a problem with the rules or members of a group in which he or she lives
> **Person against nature**—a character has a problem with an element of nature
> **Person against him/herself**—a character has a problem making decisions (usually he/she is torn between alternative choices)

Draw an X under the correct type of conflict for each sentence.

Person against person	Person against society	Person against nature	Person against him/ herself

1. The main character is not supposed to enter the medical building, yet it seems to be the only way to save her son who is ill.

2. The main character is trapped in a tornado being carried away from her family.

3. The main character is trapped on a deserted island with only one granola bar left. He can't decide if he should eat it or not. Either way, he faces dire consequences.

4. The main character is rock climbing when a severe thunderstorm unexpectedly begins.

5. The main character writes mean messages about children in her class in a secret notebook.

6. The main character has a job offer in another state, but all her friends and family are where she currently resides.

7. The main character lives in a town where all females should be covered up, but she doesn't want to wear their clothing.

8. Two main characters get into an argument.

9. The main character seems to have two voices telling him to make opposite decisions.

10. The main character must trust an owl who is normally her predator.

Name _____ Date _____

Plot It Out

PLOT

Before retelling a story, you should plot it out in sequential order. If you plot it out, then the events and conflicts explain the resolution and conclusion.

Fill in the graphic organizer with the main events from the beginning to the end of the novel you just read. Identify which part of the plot each event represents by labeling it with one of the following parts of a plot: introduction, conflict, events, turning point, resolution, falling action, conclusion.

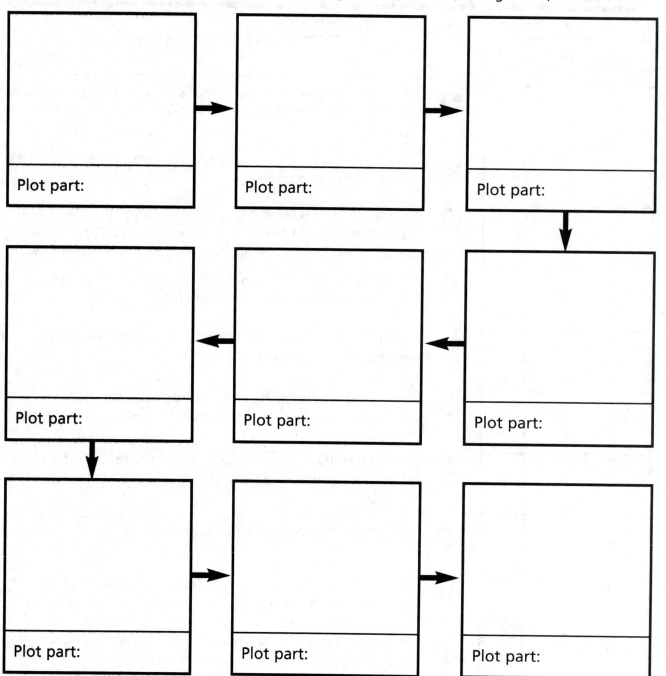

Plot part:

Plot part:

Plot part:

Plot part:

Plot part:

Plot part:

Plot part:

Plot part:

Plot part:

Reading Skills • 5–6 © 2004 Creative Teaching Press

Name _____ Date _____

Turning Points

PLOT

> Three main parts to a plot include the main event or conflict, the turning point, and the resolution.

Fill in the graphic organizer with the main event/conflict that occurred in the story you just read, the turning point that led to the solution, and the ultimate resolution of the story.

← The turning point was

_____

_____

_____

The event or conflict was ➡

_____

_____

_____

Turning Point

← The resolution was

_____

_____

_____

Reading Skills • 5-6 © 2004 Creative Teaching Press

What's the Problem?

PROBLEM AND SOLUTION

Any problem has a solution. A **problem** is something that needs to be changed for a good outcome to occur.

Write a problem that can be solved by each example. The easiest way to think of the problem is to ask yourself "Why?" for each solution. There may be many different possible problems that can be solved by each example.

1 Problem: _____
Solution: You get out the carpet cleaner.

2 Problem: _____
Solution: Alex will study for his next history test.

3 Problem: _____
Solution: Becca's mom was carefully searching for the flashlight.

4 Problem: _____
Solution: Although Suzanne usually drinks hot chocolate, today she'll settle for coffee.

5 Problem: _____
Solution: Joseph departed for the pet store.

6 Problem: _____
Solution: She was put on restriction.

7 Problem: _____
Solution: Mr. Rish gave up eating chips and candy.

8 Problem: _____
Solution: Tom pulled into the gas station.

9 Problem: _____
Solution: Lauren asked Monica to assist her in lifting the bundle of newspapers.

10 Problem: _____
Solution: The children got out of the pool.

Reading Skills • 5-6 © 2004 Creative Teaching Press

I've Got It!

PROBLEM AND SOLUTION

Any problem has a solution. A **problem** is something that needs to be changed for a good outcome to occur. A **solution** is a method of making things work out well.

Write a solution for each problem. The easiest way to think of the solution is to ask yourself "What could I do?" for each problem. There may be many different possible solutions that can be reached in each example.

1 Ian hasn't rehearsed his lines for the mock trial that will take place in two days.

2 Abby wants a new jacket like her best friend, but she hasn't saved enough money yet.

3 The concert that Luca really hoped to attend is already sold out.

4 The toddler at the birthday party is crying while looking at the clown.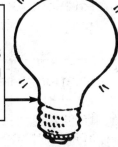

5 Melanie's lunch money seems to have mysteriously disappeared.

6 Rebecca is scared of dissecting owl pellets, but it's a classroom requirement.

7 Mrs. Yaros is late for work and there is a train crossing up ahead.

8 Mr. Zep doesn't have enough money to pay his rent.

Name _____ Date _____

Solving Problems

PROBLEM AND SOLUTION

Identify three problems that occurred in the book you just read. Write the cause of the problem.
Write the solution that was chosen to solve the problem. Explain the result. In your opinion, was
the solution the best that could have been chosen? Fill in the chart showing this information.

	Problem 1	Problem 2	Problem 3
Who/What caused the problem?			
Who created the solution?			
What was the solution?			
What was the result of the solution? (What happened then?)			
In your opinion, was that the best solution?	yes/no	yes/no	yes/no
What would you have recommended?			

Reading Skills • 5-6 © 2004 Creative Teaching Press

Name _____ Date _____

On the Other Hand

PROBLEM AND SOLUTION

Most problems have multiple solutions. Identify two problems you've encountered in your life. Write down two solutions that could have solved each problem. Explain what would have happened with each choice.

Result

_____

_____

_____

_____

_____

_____

_____

_____

_____

On one hand I could have . . .

_____

_____

_____

Problem 1

_____

_____

_____

_____

_____

_____

_____

_____

_____

On the other hand I could have . . .

_____

_____

_____

Result

_____

_____

_____

_____

_____

_____

_____

_____

_____

Result

_____

_____

_____

_____

_____

_____

_____

_____

_____

On one hand I could have . . .

_____

_____

_____

Problem 2

_____

_____

_____

_____

_____

_____

_____

_____

_____

On the other hand I could have . . .

_____

_____

_____

Result

_____

_____

_____

_____

_____

_____

_____

_____

_____

Reading Skills • 5-6 © 2004 Creative Teaching Press

Inconsistencies

REASONING

When reading, it is important to notice clues that the author provides that are inconsistent with the details. It usually means that there is a character not telling the truth or it is a form of exaggeration.

Inconsistency example: He toasted the cheese in the toaster. You can't toast cheese in a toaster since it will melt, so that's inconsistent with reality.

Read the "sentence inconsistencies." Write why they are inconsistent.

1 The family went to the zoo at midnight.

_____

2 Linda and Arthur got married on February 30th.

_____

3 Keith put out the fire with the log.

_____

4 He squeezed five oranges to make lemonade.

_____

5 The bird flew through the mountain.

_____

6 The racket broke in his soccer game.

_____

7 His batteries were dead so he turned up the volume.

_____

8 They visited the pyramids in Texas.

_____

Reading Skills • 5-6 © 2004 Creative Teaching Press

Name It!

REASONING

When reading, the author often leaves clues foreshadowing what will happen later in the book. It is important to gather the clues and make an inference and prediction each time. This process is called **deduction**.
Deductive reasoning:
batteries   bright   bulb
They are all part of a flashlight. If a character packed these items, you would expect he or she would be going camping or there was an emergency.

Read each set of clues. Write the item or place they are describing.

1. robe, gavel, courtroom _____

2. sand, water, sunshine _____

3. camping, canvas, stakes _____

4. wax, light, decorative _____

5. paper, exchange, coins _____

6. sharp, expensive, gem _____

7. keys, music, ivory _____

8. leader, elected, Washington, D.C. _____

9. jungle, predator, cat _____

10. symbol, stars, stripes _____

11. safety, red, squirt _____

12. carbonated, beverage, cavities _____

13. cob, kernels, pop _____

14. vehicle, water, vacation _____

15. prongs, handle, eat _____

Name _____ Date _____

Please Explain

REASONING

When making conclusions about what you are reading, your reasoning ability becomes important. Conclusions are based on personal knowledge, the facts in the book, and your opinions of a topic.

Answer the questions based on your reasoning and background knowledge. Answer in complete sentences.

1 Should guard rails be found on all freeways and highways?

_____

2 Are commercials informative?

_____

3 Is there any way to keep algae out of an aquarium?

_____

4 Is it important for farmers to be allowed to use pesticides to keep crop-destroying insects away?

_____

5 Are zoos important?

_____

6 Should sports stars be paid the millions of dollars they currently earn?

_____

7 Is it possible to get every citizen to obey the laws?

_____

8 Will people ever be happy with the way they look?

_____

Reading Skills • 5–6 © 2004 Creative Teaching Press

Is It Reasonable?

REASONING

Read each statement. Decide if it is reasonable or unreasonable. Circle your choice.

reasonable　　unreasonable　　**1** All one-dollar bills have the picture of George Washington on the front.

reasonable　　unreasonable　　**2** Some fractions have numerators.

reasonable　　unreasonable　　**3** All globes have continents on them.

reasonable　　unreasonable　　**4** All doughnuts have holes in the center.

reasonable　　unreasonable　　**5** Diamonds are made from aluminum.

reasonable　　unreasonable　　**6** Days are longer than nights.

reasonable　　unreasonable　　**7** Koalas are cuddly bears.

reasonable　　unreasonable　　**8** All skates have four wheels on them.

reasonable　　unreasonable　　**9** All erasers remove lead and ink.

reasonable　　unreasonable　　**10** Hurricanes only hit the Pacific Ocean.

reasonable　　unreasonable　　**11** Tornadoes hit coastal cities.

reasonable　　unreasonable　　**12** Raisins come from plums.

reasonable　　unreasonable　　**13** All grapes are green.

reasonable　　unreasonable　　**14** All locks have combinations.

reasonable　　unreasonable　　**15** All postage stamps cost money.

reasonable　　unreasonable　　**16** All magazines have advertisements.

reasonable　　unreasonable　　**17** Dragons are now extinct.

reasonable　　unreasonable　　**18** Corn grows on a vine.

Name _____ Date _____

Alike or Different

COMPARE AND CONTRAST

> To **compare** things is to see how they are the same. To **contrast** things is to see how they are different.

Compare and contrast how the following items are similar and different. List three things in each section of the Venn diagram so that you have a total of nine similarities and differences.

candle   both   light bulb

restaurant   both   grocery store

Amazing Animal Similarities

COMPARE AND CONTRAST

Fill in the graphic organizer with examples of how the animals are similar to each other. Compare each pair of animals and record at least two similarities. Be creative and thoughtful.

	Turtle	Rabbit	Bear
Cat	1. 2.	1. 2.	1. 2.
Mouse	1. 2.	1. 2.	1. 2.
Lion	1. 2.	1. 2.	1. 2.

As Different as Night and Day

COMPARE AND CONTRAST

You've heard the saying, "They're as different as night and day!" Now you get to put that to the test. Below you will find four sets of things that may seem similar at first. Contrast each pair and list at least three ways they are actually different.

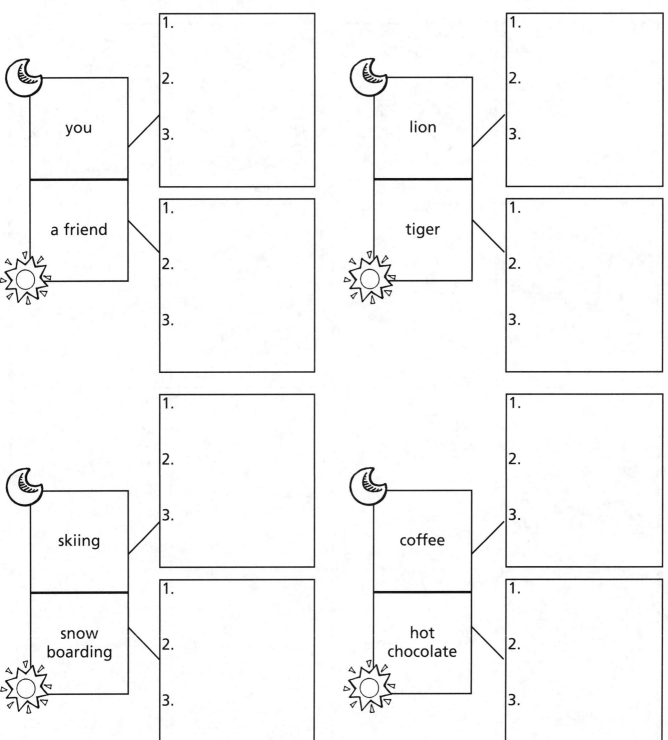

Reading Skills • 5-6 © 2004 Creative Teaching Press

Personal Connections

MAKING CONNECTIONS

Read the titles of the books and their descriptions. Read each comment made by a student in a class about a book that was just read. Match the comments to the books based on the titles and descriptions.

_____ **1** Creative Cookery—a cookbook of easy tasty treats ready in five minutes

_____ **2** Sew Happy—a craft book with samples of gifts made in a half hour using basic sewing stitches

_____ **3** Natural Disasters of North America—a book of true stories related to nature's fury

_____ **4** Fundraising for Kids—a book of ideas kids can use to raise money for needy causes

_____ **5** The Missing Camper—an adventure story about a boy who gets lost while hiking

_____ **6** The Misadventures of Hamilton—a fictional story about a hamster who escapes from its classroom cage

_____ **7** Cartoon Capers—a collection of cartoons related to funny events

_____ **8** Incredible Kid Inventions—a book of wacky inventions made by kids

a. My aunt wants to borrow the book. She made my curtains.

b. Hey! That reminds me of the cartoon on my refrigerator about the boy with the loose tooth.

c. That's like the bake sale Ashley organized for the pet shelter.

d. I've had that Pastry Pizza. It's so yummy!

e. Didn't your classroom guinea pig escape last year? It was so funny when we found it behind our bookcase!

f. That reminds me of the time I got lost on our class field trip.

g. Wow! My grandma lived through some scary hurricanes, too.

h. Some day I'll be in that book! I'm creating a Homework Machine.

Name _____ Date _____

What in the World?

MAKING CONNECTIONS

Read the short summary of the book. Answer the questions. Make connections.

 The book was about a colony of rats who were once part of a laboratory experiment. The injections of medication they received weekly for three years from the scientists make them larger, stronger, and smarter than all other rats. They also lived much longer. In fact, they never seemed to die. They could read, write, plan, organize, build, and invent things for their colony. They didn't live like other sewer rats. In fact, they lived a life of luxury not unlike humans. Electricity, fresh food, and reading materials were just a few of the things that made their daily lives pleasant. They cooperated with other species in and around the farm under which they lived. In fact, the many adventures they encounter involve these other animals. Their ultimate goal was to live without having to rely upon humans for food. They devised a clever plan for creating their own self-maintained habitat. They helped each other and tried until they succeeded.

1 What television show does this remind you a little bit of? Why?

_____

2 What location in the world could you picture the characters living in happily?

Why?_____

3 If the main characters could take a vacation, where would they enjoy going? Why?

_____

4 What newspaper comic strip does this remind you of? Why?

_____

5 What video game comes to mind when you think of the summary? Why?

_____

6 What problems would they probably face if they lived with regular rats? Why?

_____

Reading Skills • 5-6 © 2004 Creative Teaching Press

Connect the Dots

MAKING CONNECTIONS

Making a connection between new and old learning is the key to learning. A text-to-text connection compares two books. A text-to-self connection compares your life with the book you read. A text-to-world connection compares the book you read to the world (outside your own life).

Answer each question by writing the information at each dot location. Circle whether it's a t - t (text-to-text), t - s (text-to-self), or t - w (text-to-world) connection. As you fill in another connection, you will connect the dots. In the end, you will see the answer to the following question: What part of reading are the connections?

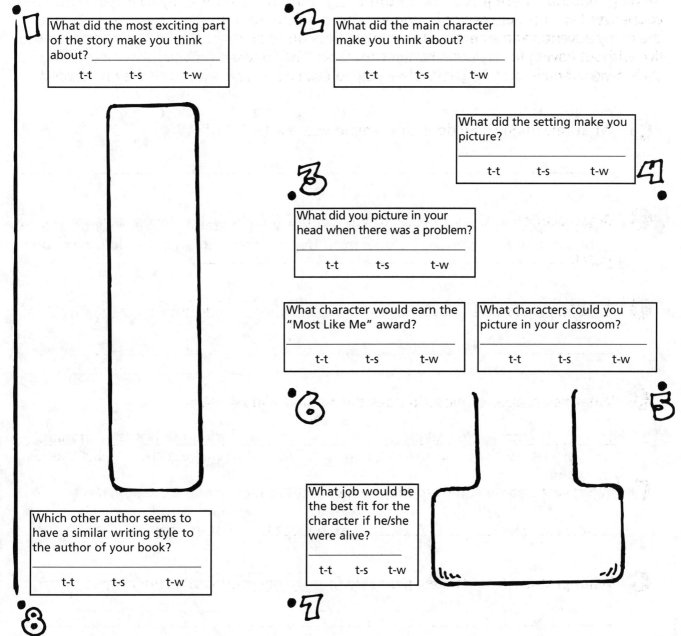

What did the most exciting part of the story make you think about? _____

t-t   t-s   t-w

What did the main character make you think about?
_____

t-t   t-s   t-w

What did the setting make you picture?
_____

t-t   t-s   t-w

What did you picture in your head when there was a problem?
_____

t-t   t-s   t-w

What character would earn the "Most Like Me" award?
_____

t-t   t-s   t-w

What characters could you picture in your classroom?
_____

t-t   t-s   t-w

What job would be the best fit for the character if he/she were alive?
_____

t-t   t-s   t-w

Which other author seems to have a similar writing style to the author of your book?
_____

t-t   t-s   t-w

The Best Choice

THEME

Read each set of details from a story. Choose the best theme. Explain why that is the best theme.

1 The main characters did kind things for each other without expecting anything in return. They led happy lives. They were respected and honored by townspeople.

    a. kindness is its own reward   **b.** be true to yourself
    c. never give up   **d.** beauty is only skin deep

_____

_____

2 When the main character was mean to his friend, he lost his friendship. He ended up lonely. He had a hard time making new friends.

    a. be true to yourself   **b.** try hard in everything you do
    c. everyone is the same on the inside   **d.** treat others the way you want to be treated

_____

_____

3 Tom didn't want to move. He always ate at the same restaurant every Sunday. He ate the same things every day. He went to bed at the same time. He didn't like any changes. He worked because he was bored.

    a. it's hard to get out of a rut   **b.** be true to yourself
    c. never give up   **d.** treat others the way you want to be treated

_____

_____

4 All of Tim's friends were making bad choices. They were trying things they shouldn't. They were trying to break rules on purpose. Tim had to make a choice—his friends or his values.

    a. be true to yourself   **b.** to be cool you have to fit in
    c. never give up   **d.** beauty is only skin deep

_____

_____

Reading Skills • 5-6 © 2004 Creative Teaching Press

Name _____ Date _____

Author Messages

THEME

The **theme** of a story is the message. It is a statement that the author feels is important enough and interesting enough to write about. The theme is the big idea, not the events of the story. However, the events can help you infer the theme. All of the elements in the novel (e.g., plot, setting, characters, events) come together to form the theme of the story.

    Example of a theme: everyone is the same on the inside
    Nonexample: love or friendship (these are topics, not themes)

Below are some topics that are often in books. To discover the theme, the reader must understand the author's message. The author's message is based on opinions and beliefs the author wants to share through writing. Pretend you are an author. You are trying to begin a new book. You are considering the topics that will develop into themes. Write the message you would want to convey to your readers based on your personal opinions.

My message would be that — love

My message would be that — family

My message would be that — environment

My message would be that — war

My message would be that — growing up

My message would be that — animals

Name _____ Date _____

Name That Theme

THEME

The theme of a story is the message. It is a statement that the author feels is important enough and interesting enough to write about. The theme is the big idea, not the events of the story.

Example of a theme: everyone is the same on the inside

Nonexample: love or friendship (these are topics, not themes)

1 The book was about a young boy who lived in a poor neighborhood. Everyone teased him throughout his years in school. Later on, he became an important doctor. He even saved the life of one of his former classmates who used to tease him as a child.

What could be the theme of the story?

_____

_____

2 The book was about a mother mouse who risked her life numerous times to save the life of her ailing son. Along the way, she discovered that her late husband had kept many secrets from her and their children. She made many new friends who offered to help and protect her and her family. When the book began, it was only her small family. By the end of the story, she had met many new people who would help her if she ever needed assistance.

What could be the theme of the story?

_____

_____

3 The book was about how a manager spoke kind words to his workers rather than always telling them what they did wrong. He focused on the positive. His workers were the most productive staff in the business. They enjoyed their jobs and were hardly ever absent.

What could be the theme of the story?

_____

_____

Reading Skills · 5-6 © 2004 Creative Teaching Press

Topic or Theme?

THEME

Read the list of topics and themes. Your goal is to identify which is which. Remember that a theme is something that is universally true. A theme is based on a topic, but takes it further. A topic is simply what the book was about. Label each example as a **topic** or **theme.**

_____ **1** friendship

_____ **2** kindness

_____ **3** Practice random acts of kindness.

_____ **4** war

_____ **5** Never give up looking for the truth.

_____ **6** honor

_____ **7** heroism

_____ **8** Treat others the way you want to be treated.

_____ **9** prejudice

_____ **10** Kindness is its own reward.

_____ **11** Never underestimate what you can do if you try.

_____ **12** success

_____ **13** courage

_____ **14** Be true to your own beliefs.

_____ **15** Beauty is only skin deep.

What do you notice most about the difference between topics and themes? Explain.

_____

_____

_____

_____

_____

Poetry
STRUCTURAL FEATURES

There are many different types of poetry. Match the type of poetry to its definition.

1 _____narrative poems

2 _____free verse

3 _____limericks

4 _____lyric poems

5 _____cinquain

a. These are five-line poems in which the first, second, and fifth lines rhyme and have three beats to the rhythm. The third and fourth lines rhyme and have two beats of rhythm. They are usually silly and humorous.

b. This type of poetry is similar to haiku. They are often about nature and do not rhyme. They have five lines. The number of syllables in successive lines are two, four, six, eight, and two.

c. These poems tell stories about real or fictional events.

d. This type of poetry began in ancient Greece. It was accompanied by the lyre. These poems are like songs and have a musical quality.

e. These do not rhyme or follow a pattern; therefore, they are the easiest to write.

Read the poem. Identify the type of poem it is.

Plain Jane

There was a young girl from Maine,
Who drove her poor mom insane.
She cut off her hair,
And wrestled a bear.
She was, by no means, a plain Jane!

Type of poem:_____

Reading Skills • 5-6 © 2004 Creative Teaching Press

Name _____ Date _____

Features of Literature

STRUCTURAL FEATURES

Folktales, fables, myths, and legends are four types of literature. Sort the statements below into the correct categories.

- usually about animals
- has a moral to share
- passed down through generations
- originally not written down
- often has a character that plays tricks on others
- is usually short and to the point
- usually involves ancient gods and goddesses
- often includes supernatural powers

- started with the Ancient Greeks
- attempts to explain the mysteries of the world
- involves heroes
- involves superhuman powers and events
- pure fiction
- no particular location in time or space
- a story from the past about a historical person
- a sacred story from the past about the universe or life

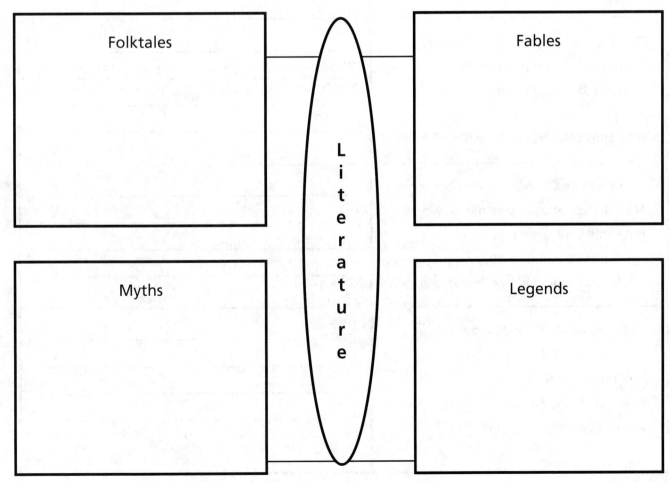

Folktales

Fables

L
i
t
e
r
a
t
u
r
e

Myths

Legends

Reading Skills • 5-6 © 2004 Creative Teaching Press

Name _____ Date _____

Lear's Limericks

Structural Features

Limericks are five-line poems in which the first, second, and fifth lines rhyme and have three beats to the rhythm. The third and fourth lines also rhyme with two beats each.

One of the most famous creators of limericks was Edward Lear (1812–1888). Read the following limericks. Write what you think he's trying to say and the overall mood you feel when reading them.

Lear's Limericks	My Interpretations & Responses
There was an Old Man on a hill, Who seldom, if ever, stood still; He ran up and down, In his grandmother's gown, Which adorned that Old Man on a hill.	_____ _____ _____ _____
There was a Young Lady whose chin, Resembled the point of a pin: So she had it made sharp and purchased a harp And played several tunes with her chin.	_____ _____ _____ _____
There was an Old Man who supposed That the street door was partially closed. But some very large rats Ate his coats and his hats While that futile old gentleman dozed.	_____ _____ _____ _____
There was an Old Lady whose folly, Induced her to sit on a holly; Whereon by a thorn, Her dress being torn, She quickly became melancholy.	_____ _____ _____ _____

Reading Skills • 5-6 © 2004 Creative Teaching Press

Name _____ Date _____

Positively Poetic
Structural Features

Read the poem by Emily Dickinson (1830–1886). Then answer the questions.

Hope is the thing with feathers
That perches in the soul,
And sings the tune without the words,
And never stops at all,

And sweetest in the gale is heard;
And sore must be the storm
That could abash the little bird
That kept so many warm.

I've heard it in the chilliest land,
And on the strangest sea;
Yet, never, in extremity,
It asked a crumb of me.

1 What does Emily Dickinson compare with hope?

_____

_____

2 What is the overall tone of this poem?

_____

_____

3 What is her message?

_____

_____

4 Draw a picture of the image you see when rereading this poem.

Name _____   Date _____

Sort It Out

ORGANIZED COMPREHENSION

After reading many details, it is important to organize the information into chunks for long-term recall. This is an especially important study technique used with textbook reading.

Read the paragraph. Fill in the sorting map.

Mammals fit into three different categories: herbivores, carnivores, and omnivores. Herbivores are animals that primarily rely upon grains and grasses for their nutritional value. They have to continuously eat, since their bodies typically do not store as much energy for future use as carnivores. Herbivores include sheep, horses, rabbits, and snails. Carnivores are animals that eat meat for energy. They can store this energy for long periods of time, so they don't typically eat all day like the herbivores. Carnivores are usually predators in the wild. They include wolves, cheetahs, eagles, and even some insects. The dragonfly is a carnivore that is constantly hunting for other insects. Omnivores are animals that eat both plants and animals. One example of an omnivore is a chicken, which eats both seeds and worms. Another omnivore is the chimpanzee. Chimpanzees will eat fruit, leaves, palm nuts, stems, ants, bird eggs, and termites. These three types of eaters comprise all of the mammals on earth.

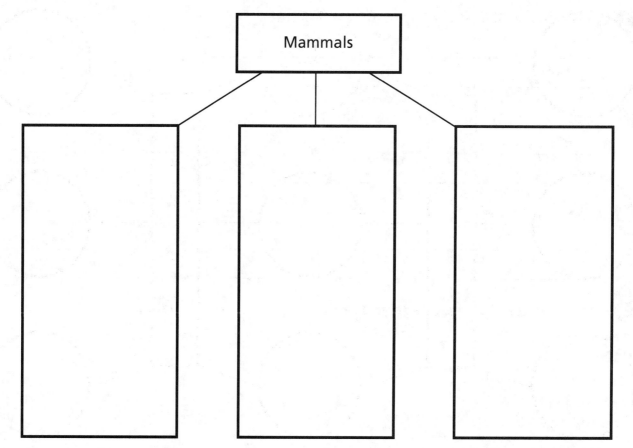

Get Organized

ORGANIZED COMPREHENSION

A **concept map** is particularly helpful when comparing two things that have overlapping characteristics.

Read the paragraph. Fill in the bubble comparison chart.

The states of California and New York are similar in many ways. They both have highly populated major cities. These states are home to most of the movie and television industries. They also have some of the most expensive homes in the United States. Both states have big cities with crowded streets and traffic problems. However, they also have beautiful countryside as well. Although the similarities make the two states popular vacation spots, there are also many differences. The capital of California, Sacramento, has roughly three times the number of people living there than the capital of New York (Albany). As far as natural disasters are concerned, earthquakes are more likely in California than New York. However, the average rainfall in the capital cities is roughly three times more rain in Albany than in Sacramento. New York is also famous for its snowstorms, which may or may not draw more visitors. Whether a visitor travels to New York or to California, he or she is bound to have an eventful trip.

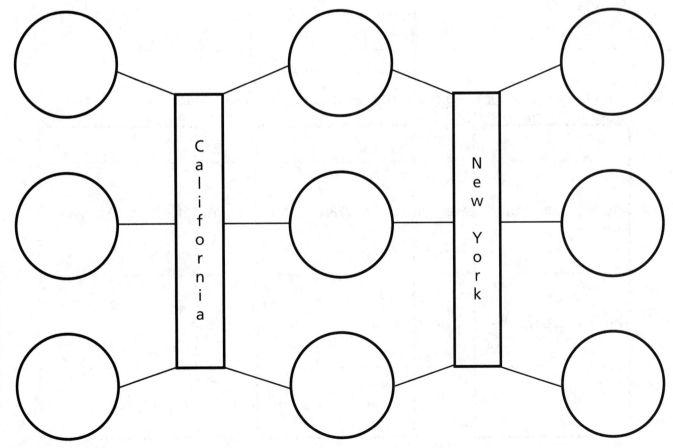

Reading Skills • 5-6 © 2004 Creative Teaching Press

Catch Phrases

ORGANIZED COMPREHENSION

Sometimes the details do not seem to relate to a category or are difficult to remember. One strategy is to generate a "catch phrase" that will trigger your memory to recall what you read. Examples: The points on a compass in order: North, South, East, West. Many people remember this by the phrase "Never Eat Soggy Waffles."

Write a catch phrase for learning the following information.

1 The lines of the treble musical staff: E, G, B, D,F

_____

2 The parts of the solar system: comets, sun, asteroids, planets, meteors

_____

3 The continents: North America, South America, Europe, Asia, Australia, Africa, Antarctica

_____

4 The planets in order from the sun: Mercury, Venus, Earth, Mars, Jupiter, Saturn, Uranus, Neptune, Pluto

_____

5 The first five United States Presidents: Washington, Adams, Jefferson, Madison, Monroe

_____

6 The five Great Lakes: Huron, Ontario, Michigan, Erie, Superior

_____

Acronyms
Organized Comprehension

Sometimes you must memorize details that are difficult to recall. One strategy that works well is to create an acronym. An **acronym** is an abbreviation in which each letter represents a word that you need to recall. The reason it works so well is that you have "chunked" the information for recall. If you can remember the first letter, that triggers your memory, and you are more likely to remember the word.

Examples: You need to remember the five Great Lakes. That's difficult unless you remember the acronym HOMES. Each letter in HOMES represents a lake. The Great Lakes are Huron, Ontario, Michigan, Erie, and Superior.

Below are some common acronyms. Write down what each letter represents.

1 SWAT _____ _____ _____ _____

2 PTA _____ _____ _____

3 NATO _____ _____ _____ _____

4 NASA _____ _____ _____ _____

5 FDA _____ _____ _____

6 FBI _____ _____ _____

7 NBA _____ _____ _____

8 CIA _____ _____ _____

9 CDC _____ _____ _____

10 NYSE _____ _____ _____ _____

11 DMV _____ _____ _____

12 FCC _____ _____ _____

13 ATV _____ _____ _____

14 USDA _____ _____ _____ _____

15 UN _____ _____

Name _____ Date _____

Name That Activity
INFERENCES

Read each statement. Make inferences to determine which activity the statement is telling you about. Write the letter of the matching activity.

_____ **1** The bat is near the dugout.   **a.** tennis

_____ **2** You can buy a new lace at the rink.   **b.** fishing

_____ **3** She splashed around and dove to the bottom.   **c.** golf

_____ **4** He knocked down all the pins the first time.   **d.** soccer

_____ **5** I dropped my racket when the serve hit the net.   **e.** drawing

_____ **6** She dealt three clubs and a diamond.   **f.** baseball

_____ **7** I am entered in the 200 meter dash.   **g.** surfing the Internet

_____ **8** When someone touches you, you are it!   **h.** skating

_____ **9** The girl did a flip off the balance beam.   **i.** swimming

_____ **10** The goalie can only touch the ball with his hands.   **j.** star gazing

_____ **11** The puck crossed the centerline on the ice.   **k.** running

_____ **12** The player shot the ball from the free throw line.   **l.** hockey

_____ **13** I usually ride after school, but my chain fell off.   **m.** watching television

_____ **14** My dad hit a hole-in-one on the fourth hole.   **n.** basketball

_____ **15** The boy adjusted his telescope by 45 degrees.   **o.** bowling

_____ **16** The quarterback passed the ball to the receiver.   **p.** football

_____ **17** My uncle puts the bait on my hook for me.   **q.** playing cards

_____ **18** I typed in the URL and waited for it to load.   **r.** bike riding

_____ **19** He used the remote to change the channel.   **s.** gymnastics

_____ **20** She shaded some areas darker using her pencil.   **t.** tag

Reading Skills • 5–6 © 2004 Creative Teaching Press

What Do You Think?

INFERENCES

An **inference** is something you assume to be true based on the reading, your judgments, and logical thinking skills. This is an important life skill that helps in good decision making.

Read each set of statements. Decide which would be the most accurate inference using all of the stated facts, your judgments, and logical thinking. Write a checkmark on the line next to the best inference.

1 The news included some comparisons of the east coast with the west coast. Weather maps were used to support the statements made by the spokesperson. Some people were trapped in their homes for days. Stores and businesses were closed for an undetermined length of time.

___ It was a national holiday.
___ There was a terrible firestorm.
___ The snowstorm was the worst in ten years.

2 Garrett was test driving a new automobile. He was impressed by the many air bags. He barely listened as the salesperson spoke of the car's sleek style and speed capability.

___ He was primarily concerned with the safety of a vehicle.
___ He wanted to look good to his friends.
___ He was mostly concerned about the gas mileage and repair history.

3 He enjoyed his job very much since he got to help people in need. He had a huge collection of keys. His phone number could be found in the phone book.

___ He was a police officer.
___ He was a valet attendant at a restaurant.
___ He was a locksmith.

4 It enjoyed laying around most of the day. It had a bad reputation for being lazy. It would eat almost anything.

___ It was a cow.
___ It was a goat.
___ It was a pig.

Name ______________________ Date ______________________

Cartoon Capers

Inferences

Look at the cartoon. Decide what is happening using all of the clues in the picture. Fill in the information.

Where?

____
____
____
____
____

Who?

____
____
____
____
____

How?

____
____
____
____
____

Why?

____
____
____
____
____

When?

____
____
____
____
____

What?

____
____
____
____
____

Reading Skills • 5-6 © 2004 Creative Teaching Press

Favorite Sports

Inferences

> An **inference** is something you assume to be true based on the reading, your judgments, and logical thinking skills. Inferences are a form of deduction. You take what you know, read the clues, and think about what could be possible based on the facts. Eliminating what is not possible is the key.

Fill in the deduction logic puzzle by reading each clue. When you reach some information that tells you a person doesn't like a certain sport, then put an "X" in that box. When you make an inference about what sport each person does play based on the facts and elimination, then color in that box. If a box is colored to represent "yes," then all other boxes in that column and row should have an "X" in them.

	Pauli	Bob	Deanne	Paul
soccer				
basketball				
tennis				
volleyball				

Clues to base your inferences on:

1. To prepare for his sport, Bob runs two miles every day.

2. Since Pauli is right handed, she couldn't play her sport when she broke her right arm.

3. Deanne's team is so good that they often end up with a final score that breaks 100!

4. The person who uses a racket in her sport practices every day.

5. Paul loves to play his sport at the beach.

Reading Skills • 5-6 © 2004 Creative Teaching Press

Name _____   Date _____

What's Next?

INFERENCES

An **inference** is something you assume to be true based on the reading, your judgments, and logical thinking skills.

Read the situations. Use the word clues, background knowledge, and your own experiences to make an inference about what will happen next.

1 The little girl was walking barefoot through the grass. A beehive was two feet away. She heard a beautiful buzzing noise. Since she was an inquisitive little girl, she wanted to see where the amazing buzzing was coming from.

_____

_____

2 The fertile soil around the base of the mountain had allowed the fragrant flowers to bloom year round. Suddenly, there was smoke billowing out of the top of the mountain. People began running and screaming!

_____

_____

3 She felt so terrible that she forgot her friend's birthday. What could she possibly do? It was too late to go to the store and get a present since they closed hours ago. Then the solution simply popped into her head.

_____

_____

4 The science teacher told her students that they could put the baking soil into the bottle of vinegar. She reminded them to leave their safety goggles on at all times.

_____

_____

5 Luis' mom began packing their belongings. It was moving day and he would begin attending his new school three days later. He saw his good friend Evan.

_____

_____

Reading Skills • 5-6 © 2004 Creative Teaching Press

Answer Key

Unfinished Words (page 5)

1. hit the sack
2. in hot water
3. fit like a glove
4. brush up on
5. sleep on it
6. up to something
7. raining cats and dogs
8. blow your top
9. on the ball

Puzzling Proverbs (page 6)

Across

1. news
3. stone
4. dull
6. early
7. parted
8. curiosity
9. skin
11. cover

Down

2. son
3. saved
5. louder
7. play
8. choosers
10. silver

Sensational Similes (page 7)

Answers will vary. Possible answers include:

1. foghorn, speaker
2. building, tree
3. bee, fly
4. sandpaper
5. rainbow, box of crayons
6. molasses
7. roses
8. pit, room at midnight
9. laying bricks, lifting weights
10. an airplane, a jet

11. a horse
12. jar of red peppers, jalapeno
13. locker room, pig sty
14. cotton
15. an ox, a mule
16. an eel

What Are You Talking About? (page 8)

1. whale sang; He was excited.
2. homework calling; It was time to do her homework.
3. water danced; The water was splashing all around the boat.
4. glasses begging; The glasses needed to be on.
5. wind knocked; It was very windy outside and the noise woke her up.
6. trash truck opened its mouth and swallowed; The trash truck collected the trash.

You've Got to Be Kidding! (page 9)

1. cried a river of tears; cried hard
2. a million times; many times
3. sleep for a year; sleep a long time
4. weigh a ton; are heavy
5. take her all day; take a long time
6. where her face begins or ends; the makeup covers her entire face
7. even insects won't live there; it's deserted
8. a thousand times a day; throughout the day
9. books have Roman numerals instead of page numbers; old and tattered books
10. a hundred years old; I'll be in the garden most of the day

In the News (page 10)

The following text should be underlined and labeled with **H**:

go on forever
off to a running start
spinning in their shoes
what hit them
too hot to handle
all the way to Japan
The following items should be underlined and labeled with **S**:
as organized as a teacher's desk
as powerful as a lion
as sly as a fox
as quick as lightning
The following items should be underlined and labeled with **P**:
hoop cheering
ball begging

Homophones (page 11)

1. their
2. banned
3. blew
4. board
5. cell
6. tail
7. waste
8. fourth
9. seam
10. hoarse
11. pact
12. peace
13. pier
14. witch
15. peak

Puzzled? (page 12)

Across

1. plane
2. steak
3. stake
4. night
5. sweet
6. weight
7. which
8. there

Down
1. peddle
3. sealing
5. suite
9. wait
10. knight
11. witch
12. their

All Mixed Up (page 13)

(The first word should be crossed out with the second word in its place)
1. ant—aunt, blue—blew, bored—board, plain—plane
2. hall—haul, hey—hay, mist—missed
3. mussel—muscle, flours—flowers
4. mourning—morning, witch—which, ware—wear
5. their—there, wood—would
6. there—their, fined—find
7. hair—hare, threw—through
8. wait—weight
9. weather—whether
10. mite—might, stake—steak, knight—night

Missing Words (page 14)

1. rain
2. reign
3. oar
4. ore
5. hire
6. higher
7. heard
8. herd
9. hole
10. whole
11. hear
12. here
13. knew
14. new
15. chilly
16. chili

Thinking Out of the Box (page 15)

Answers will vary. Possible answers include:

similar—same, alike, related, identical

hilarious—comical, amusing, hysterical, funny

solicit—peddle, ask, beg, plead

duplicate—copy, reproduce, replicate, clone

challenging—difficult, hard, tough, demanding

query—ask, inquire, request, question

disrupt—interrupt, interfere, disturb, bother

cordial—kind, friendly, courteous, pleasant

evil—malevolent, cruel, mean, wicked

In Other Words . . . (page 16)

1. irritated
2. pleased
3. live
4. mistakes
5. destroyed
6. quickly
7. bickered
8. empty
9. finishing
10. escort
11. detests
12. excited

Synonym Sandwiches (page 17)

Each sandwich should have the following two words on the bread:
1. enormous, gigantic
2. accompany, meet
3. grateful, appreciative
4. amount, total
5. funny, hilarious
6. nippy, cool
7. disappeared, dissipated

8. selected, picked
9. irritate, agitate
10. dangerous, detrimental

That's Not What I Said (page 18)

1. arrives
2. unsure
3. pleased
4. climb
5. fragile
6. lost
7. slowly
8. frightening
9. show
10. lazy
11. rarely
12. started

Antonym Match-Up (page 19)

1. n
2. e
3. h
4. d
5. b
6. m
7. g
8. l
9. c
10. j
11. k
12. i
13. a
14. f
15. o

Opposites Attract (page 20)

Answers will vary but must include antonyms. Possible answers include:
1. rude, impolite
2. finish, complete
3. old, used
4. fix, repair
5. answer, reply
6. positive, certain
7. disappear, erase

8. arrive, come

Secret Code (page 21)

1. doctor
2. polite
3. think
4. relaxing
5. stop
6. complain
7. construct
8. draw
9. friend
10. gullible
11. boring
12. thirsty

Secret code: You can do analogies well!

Match It Up (page 22)

1. fair
2. filthy
3. energized
4. microscopic
5. starve
6. purchase
7. common
8. allow
9. courage
10. novice
11. foolish
12. hoard
13. untruthful
14. cheerful
15. tiresome

Unscramble It! (page 23)

1. year
2. keyboard
3. letter
4. soldier
5. supreme court
6. diameter
7. orchestra
8. flock
9. stanza

10. plant
11. sentence
12. pack
13. wardrobe
14. toilet
15. quarterback

Analyze This! (page 24)

Answers will vary. Possible answers include:

1. ruby
2. sly
3. white
4. bird
5. recipe
6. pool
7. trash
8. benevolent
9. humid
10. cast
11. chicken
12. movie
13. exercise
14. boat
15. fish
16. cure

Fill In the Blanks (page 25)

1. d
2. a
3. c
4. b
5. c
6. b

What Does It Mean? (page 26)

Answers may vary. Possible answers include:

1. assumed—figured out
2. gasping—searching for air
3. misgivings—uncertainty
4. erratically—crazy driving all over the road
5. glimpse—a small piece
6. urgency—rushed

7. vague—unclear
8. derived—got out of it

Sentence Sense (page 27)

1. descent
2. confident
3. already
4. conscious
5. effect
6. adapt
7. eliminate
8. except
9. compliments
10. eluded
11. through
12. desert
13. stationary
14. lay
15. route

You Be the Dictionary (page 28)

Answers will vary. Possible answers include:

1. a place where dirty clothes are placed before they are washed
2. a tool used to protect the head and body from rain
3. a tool used to measure length
4. a paper folded to hold something that needs to be mailed
5. a piece of reflective glass that shows the image in reverse
6. a tool used to attach papers with a piece of metal
7. an organ vital to life that pumps blood throughout the body
8. an animal that flies
9. an item made out of wood or metal with steps that is used for climbing
10. a tool used to shine in areas that are dark
11. a tool used by a judge to get the attention of the members in the courtroom

12. a machine that people use to walk or run on
13. a tool used in navigation or traveling that helps a person locate directions
14. a commercial or sales pitch
15. a liquid used to make hands softer

Prefix Match-Up (page 29)

1. g
2. c
3. e
4. f
5. k
6. h
7. a
8. l
9. i
10. b
11. j
12. d

Personal Opinion Questions (page 30)

Answers will vary.

Are You Serious? (page 31)

1. literal
2. rhetorical
3. literal
4. rhetorical
5. rhetorical
6. literal
7. rhetorical
8. rhetorical
9. literal
10. literal
11. rhetorical
12. literal
13. literal
14. rhetorical
15. rhetorical

Always, Sometimes, Never (page 32)

1. always
2. never
3. sometimes
4. never
5. sometimes
6. sometimes
7. sometimes
8. always
9. sometimes
10. always
11. always
12. sometimes
13. sometimes
14. always
15. sometimes
16. always
17. sometimes
18. sometimes

You're the Teacher (page 33)

Answers will vary but should include well-written *who, what, when, where, why,* and *how* questions in complete sentences based on the paragraph.

You're the Teacher Again (page 34)

Answers will vary but should include well-written *who, what, when, where, why,* and *how* questions in complete sentences based on the paragraph.

Marshmallow Cereal Bars (page 35)

1. HIGH
2. two cups of peanuts
3. it melts
4. 12 x 8 in.
5. butter, marshmallows, peanut butter, cereal, peanuts
6. cool them in the refrigerator
7. quarter cup
8. Depends on class size but most likely not enough since the recipe only makes 12 bars.

Handy Dandy Card Holder (page 36)

1. In order to make the card holder, you need two clear plastic lids, a metal brad, and decorative materials.
2. The plastic lids need to be clear so you can see the cards through them.
3. I think the outside should be decorated with permanent marker because sweaty hands will wipe off washable marker. (Answers may vary)
4. If the lids were different sizes the cards wouldn't stay in.
5. any answer that hints on the fact that the cards have a fixed size and the two lids must press against each other

Pictures will vary but should resemble the holder described in the text.

What's the Answer? (page 37)

Montana

Hawaiian Pizza (page 38)

1. loaf of French bread, pizza sauce, Canadian bacon, one bell pepper, one can of pineapple, mozarella cheese
2. Cut the loaf in half lengthwise.
3. bacon, bell pepper, pineapple, cheese
4. bacon, bell pepper, pineapple, cheese
5. It melts faster. (answers may vary)
6. four
7. It's bigger than the loaf of bread. (answers may vary)
8. Slice it in half and serve.

Four in Four (page 39)

Answers will vary. Most common

responses:

Money—euro, pound, yen, dollar

Italian Food—lasagna, brushetta, spaghetti, pizza

Fruit—pear, cranberry, orange, plum

Sea Life—tuna, marlin, lobster, sea urchin

Great Lakes—Erie, Huron, Ontario, Superior, Michigan

Presidents—Lincoln, Roosevelt, Carter, Bush

Continents—Asia, Africa, South America, Europe

Countries—Portugal, Spain, Netherlands, Canada

Classes—music, science, math, history

Trains—rail, caboose, engine, car

Shades of Blue—aquamarine, turquoise, sky, slate

Parts of a Computer—keyboard, mouse, disk drive, monitor

Elimination (page 40)

1. throw—not a sport
2. building—not a room
3. wet—not a beverage
4. Perot—not a president
5. Aldrich—not an explorer
6. menu—not something you renew
7. bicycle—not something you inflate
8. fur—not something strong
9. smile—not an emotion

A Full House (page 41)

Answers will vary. Possible answers include:

1. states—Alabama, Alaska, Arizona, Arkansas
2. entertainment places—theme park, circus, theater, concert hall
3. sports—basketball, baseball, soccer, tennis
4. things that are round—clock, merry-go-round, CD, record
5. sloppy things—desks, junk drawers, pig sty, farmer's pants
6. warm things—bathtub, terrycloth robe, sunshine, mittens
7. amazing books—Mrs. Frisby, Nancy Drew, From the Mixed Up Files, The City of Gold and Lead
8. containers—pencil box, shoe box, retainer canister, soda can
9. household appliances—hair dryer, washing machine, coffee maker, refrigerator
10. vacation destinations—Hawaii, Tahiti, Italy, London
11. acronyms—PTA, FBI, SWAT, ATV
12. mammals—dogs, horse, cats, lions

The Outline (page 42)

A Balanced Diet

I. Dairy Group
   A. milk
   B. cheese
   C. yogurt
II. Meat Group
   A. poultry
   B. beef
   C. fish
   D. dried beans
III. Breads and Cereals
   A. pasta
   B. tortillas
   C. macaroni
IV. Vegetable Group
   A. broccoli
   B. asparagus
   C. carrots
   D. brussel sprouts
V. Fruit Group
   A. raspberries
   B. pears

What Category? (page 43)

1. games
2. dogs
3. dances
4. artists
5. flowers
6. sports
7. instruments
8. clothes
9. things you read
10. presidents
11. things that measure
12. composers

The Big Idea (page 44)

1. computer items
2. money
3. presidents
4. Great Lakes
5. compass points or directions
6. vegetables
7. sports
8. occupations
9. beverages
10. languages or nationalities
11. reptiles
12. math terms
13. weather words
14. flavors
15. continents

How Supportive Are You? (page 45)

The following should be checked off:

1. b, d, f
2. b, d, e
3. a, c, e
4. a, b, c, d

Prove It! (page 46)

Answers will vary but must have matching supportive details underlined.

1. Arthropods are invertebrates—hard exoskeleton, bugs, bodies made of sections
2. The Great Depression caused

financial hardship—longest period of unemployment, no jobs, slow business growth, businesses failed

Main Idea and Details (page 47)

Main Idea: Many computer-related jobs are now available.

Details:

* The jobs currently available include web page designers, online auction resellers, computer technicians, software developers, and computer engineers.
* Someday, hospitals could be completely run by computers and robots.
* Computer engineers are developing different ways that computers can help disabled and stroke victims as well as doctors and nurses.

Paired Up (page 48)

Answers will vary. Possible answers include:

1. girls
2. eggs
3. dog
4. pencil
5. take
6. health
7. pepper
8. go
9. spoon
10. bad
11. answers
12. error
13. sister
14. new
15. cookies
16. cents
17. popcorn
18. stripes
19. princess
20. hare
25. thin
22. poorer
23. stones
24. crackers
25. cheese

Get Logical! (page 49)

Answers will vary but should be based on the text.

Predictions Aren't Perfect (page 50)

Answers will vary.

Television Titles (page 51)

Answers will vary.

Get to Know the Character (page 52)

1. True
2. False
3. True
4. True
5. True
6. False
7. False
8. True
9. False
10. False

Casting Call (page 53)

1. b
2. f
3. k
4. j
5. n
6. g
7. h
8. i
9. e
10. a
11. o
12. l
13. c
14. m
15. d

A Feel for the Character (page 54)

1. hope
2. excitement
3. worry
4. disgust
5. despair
6. frustration
7. fear
8. happiness
9. nervousness
10. anger

Traits on Plates (page 55)

Answers will vary. Possible answers include:

1. in2risk—risk taker, daring
2. bravboy—risk taker, not afraid of challenges
3. imsmart—intelligent, educated
4. icuhlp2—helpful, compassionate, giving
5. nvrgvup—persistent, keeps on trying
6. urkind2—kindness, courteous, polite, friendly
7. imonist—honest, trustworthy, kind
8. neverl8—punctual, always on time, respectful
9. apolit1—courteous, polite, cordial
10. icare4u—kind, helpful, compassionate

Matching Settings (page 56)

1. e
2. j
3. h
4. c
5. d
6. b
7. f
8. i
9. g

10. a

Get in the Mood (page 57)

Answers will vary.

It's in the Details (page 58)

Answers will vary.

Ready on the Set (page 59)

1. bedroom
2. playground
3. street in front of house
4. car driving somewhere
5. kitchen
6. Saturday morning on the block
7. a toddler's room
8. bedroom

What's Next? (page 60)

barbecue: 2, 1, 5, 3, 4
soup: 4, 2, 3, 1, 5
dog: 1, 2, 4, 5, 3
airplane: 5, 2, 1, 3, 4
cake: 2, 1, 3, 5, 4

Sequence Your Life (page 61)

Answers will vary.

Comics (page 62)

1. 1,4,2,3
2. 3,4,1,2
3. 3,2,4,1
4. 4,3,2,1

The Life of Bill Gates (page 63)

Answers will vary. Possible answers include:
born October 28, 1955
bored in school
private school
fell in love with computers
developed computer programs
met Paul Allen
created company called Traf-O-Data
developed school software program for arranging classes
went to Harvard
left Harvard for business opportunities
billionaire at 31
created Microsoft®

Which Meaning Makes Sense? (page 64)

1. b
2. b
3. b
4. b
5. b
6. b
7. b
8. b
9. b
10. a

Not So Tricky After All (page 65)

Answers will vary. Possible answers include:

1. moving your hand or body to show what you are thinking or feeling
2. to move from a higher place to a lower one
3. divided
4. thought about
5. used to, familiar with
6. held, kept in
7. hard to understand
8. the guilty ones

Get to the Root of the Matter (page 66)

1. transport = trans + port = to carry across
2. coexist = co + exist = to stay/live together
3. bisect = bi + sect = to cut into two sections
4. transmit = trans + mit = to send across
5. biped = bi + ped = two feet
6. revive = re + vive = to bring to life again
7. transect = trans + sect = to cut across
8. export = ex + port = to carry out
9. remit = re + mit = to send again
10. rejoin = re + join = to put together again

Context Clues Crossword (page 67)

Across
2. optimistic
5. enthusiasm
7. illusion
9. concoction
11. ecstatic
13. exhilarating

Down
1. context
3. dispute
4. justice
6. predicament
8. velocity
10. abundance

Context Clues (page 68)

Answers will vary. Possible answers for dictionary definitions include:
1. jurisdiction—area in which he works and rules
2. justify—prove
3. maneuver—move around
4. anticlimatic—disappointing
5. benefactor—kind person who donated money

Why Did It Happen? (page 69)

Additional causes will vary.
1. a, c
2. a, b
3. b, c
4. a, b
5. a, c

What Happened? (page 70)

1. bad grades
2. flooded
3. floated
4. rescued
5. evacuated
6. debt
7. broke her arm
8. used his inhaler

What and Why? (page 71)

1. broke her arm, dad got to do the cooking
2. broke off his leash, running through the neighborhood
3. it is remodeling and expanding, bagel shop was closed
4. his computer crashed, ended up in a computer store
5. daily hamburgers, giving her high cholesterol
6. his books are adored, he became a billionaire
7. electricity went out, movie let out early
8. it was her birthday, ran to the door to get the package
9. he was hungry, nibbled on dandelion greens
10. cap left open all weekend, glue dried out
11. it was ruined in the hurricane, had to demolish the house
12. to spend more time with her family, quit her job
13. daily arguments, mother took it away
14. increased level of air pollution, large trucks pay higher fees
15. eating five handfuls of jelly beans, had a stomachache

The Good and the Bad of It All (page 72)

Answers will vary but should include both positive and negative effects.

Find the Cause or Effect (page 73)

Cause
1. Adam planted tomato seeds.
2. He watered the seeds every day.
3. He put the pot in sunlight and added fertilizer to the soil.

Effect
4. I needed my sunglasses.
5. I wore shorts.

Cause
6. Erin made the winning basket.

Effect
7. The crowd cheered.
8. The team won for the first time.
9. Erin was named Most Valuable Player.

Alluring Advertisements (page 74)

Another satisfied customer! We at Phillips Automotive know how much you care about buying a quality car. That's why we're #1 in customer satisfaction. We make the best cars and sell them at the best prices. You won't find a better car in any state! If you want more car for your money, then hustle on down to Phillips Automotive! We care about you. We care about the car you drive. We have over 3,000 cars ready for you to test drive. Hurry! Cars are moving fast! Just ask for me—Jeff Phillips. I'll give you what you deserve!

Hey kids! You know how much your family cares about your safety. Well, we do too! We've designed the all new Cool Cap! Everyone on your block wants to have one. Don't be left out. Go to your local sports shop and ask for the Cool Cap. You'll be the coolest kid on your block and you'll be safe!

Girl—Wow! That's the best tasting water in the world! It's hard to believe I'm taking my vitamins! Look Dad! I'm done. I can't wait to see what flavor I get tomorrow.
Dad—I'm so proud of you! To think that we used to argue over vitamins. That's all over now thanks to Aguavites! There's no better way to take vitamins. That's why every parent in the world is trying new Aguavites. It gets everyone's day off to a great start.

It's the newest kitty craze! Every cat on your block will be at your door trying to get in when you fill your cat's bowl with Tasty Treats Cat Food. That's right, your cat will thank you every day for the delicious treat. Only you will know that it's not a treat—it's his food! There's not a cat who doesn't love Tasty Treats Cat Food. So . . . what are you waiting for? Run out and get some Tasty Treats Cat Food right away. Your cat will be healthier and happier. You'll know that you're giving your cat the best food on the market. Look for Tasty Treats Cat Food in the pet food aisle of your local pet store. Hurry! The stores are running out fast!

Unscrambled Hints (page 75)

seems, think, best, all, believe, many, better, worst, awful, everyone

1. everyone
2. think
3. better
4. worst, ever
5. seems, harder
6. best
7. believe, better
8. think, more
9. awful
10. all, should

For Sale (page 76)

Answers will vary.

The Flip Side (page 77)

Answers will vary. Possible answers include:

1. My teacher is smart.
2. My school doesn't have a parachute.
3. Computers cost more than televisions.
4. I don't like cauliflower.
5. I am lazy in high humidity.
6. Science involves experiments.
7. Computers can be useful in classrooms.
8. I think birds migrate in winter.
9. It looks like the sports arena may be sold out.
10. Going up in altitude seems to make it harder for me to breathe.
11. It seems like regular coffee has caffeine.
12. It seems like solar energy makes some calculators work.
13. I think a ruler measures inches or centimeters.
14. I don't think penguins can fly.

Key Points (page 78)

Summaries will vary.

Big Ideas of a Summary (page 79)

1. The summary should be written in your own words.
2. The most important information should be presented first.
3. Only main ideas and important details should be included.
4. The most important characters should be named.
5. There should be vocabulary directly from the reading in the summary.
6. The summary should be short but complete.
7. The summary should be clear.
8. There should not be any of your opinions in the summary.

Comical Summaries (page 80)

Summaries will vary.

Summarize Anything (page 81)

Answers will vary.

Plot Parts (page 82)

1. g
2. f
3. b
4. c
5. e
6. d
7. a

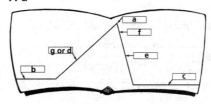

Conflicts (page 83)

1. person against society
2. person against nature
3. person against self
4. person against nature
5. person against society
6. person against self
7. person against society
8. person against person
9. person against self
10. person against self

Plot It Out (page 84)

Answers will vary.

Turning Points (page 85)

Answers will vary.

What's the Problem? (page 86)

Answers will vary. Possible answers include:

1. William spilled coffee on the carpet.
2. Alex got a D on his history test.
3. There was a power outage at the house.
4. We ran out of hot chocolate mix.
5. Joseph's new puppy needed a food bowl and a pillow to sleep on.
6. Caroline had diabetes and was eating too much sugar.
7. Mr. Rish was overweight.
8. The gas tank was almost empty.
9. Lauren could not lift all of the newspapers.
10. Someone poured too much chlorine in the pool.

I've Got It! (page 87)

Answers will vary. Possible answers include:

1. Ian will spend the next two days rehearsing his lines.
2. Abby will save money and buy the jacket when she has saved enough.
3. Luca will try to buy tickets for the next concert.
4. The toddler's mother takes him into another room, away from the clown.
5. Melanie tells her teacher about the situation.
6. Rebecca explains her fears to the teacher so the teacher asks a classmate to help Rebecca.
7. Mrs. Yaro calls her boss and explains the situation.
8. Mr. Zep borrows money from his mother.

Solving Problems (page 88)

Answers will vary.

On the Other Hand (page 89)

Answers will vary.

Inconsistencies (page 90)

1. zoos aren't open at midnight
2. inaccurate date
3. logs build fires
4. oranges make orange juice not lemonade
5. birds fly around mountains
6. rackets aren't used in soccer
7. with dead batteries volume doesn't work
8. pyramids aren't in Texas

Name It! (page 91)

Answers will vary. Possible answers include:

1. judge
2. ocean
3. tent
4. candle
5. money
6. diamond
7. piano
8. president
9. tiger, lion, or jaguar
10. flag
11. fire extinguisher
12. soda
13. corn
14. boat
15. fork

Please Explain (page 92)

Answers will vary.

Is It Reasonable? (page 93)

1. reasonable
2. unreasonable—all fractions have numerators
3. reasonable
4. unreasonable—the doughnut holes are doughnuts without holes
5. unreasonable—aluminum is a metal; diamonds are stones
6. unreasonable—depends on time of year
7. unreasonable—technically koalas are not bears
8. unreasonable—inline skates
9. unreasonable—some do, some don't
10. unreasonable—Atlantic Ocean more than Pacific
11. unreasonable—Tornado Alley is through center of America
12. unreasonable—prunes
13. unreasonable—purple and red grapes
14. unreasonable—keys
15. reasonable
16. unreasonable—only those that want the income
17. unreasonable—never lived; therefore can't be extinct
18. unreasonable—grapes on a vine

Alike or Different (page 94)

Answers will vary.

Amazing Animal Similarities (page 95)

Answers will vary.

As Different as Night and Day (page 96)

Answers will vary.

Personal Connections (page 97)

1. d
2. a
3. g
4. c
5. f
6. e
7. b
8. h

What in the World? (page 98)

Answers will vary. Possible answers include:

1. rat cartoon or TV show; reasons vary
2. any comfortable environment; reasons vary
3. somewhere with electricity, fresh food, comfort; reasons vary
4. any animal strip; reasons vary
5. varies with individual
6. different level of intelligence, different lifestyle, different foods, lack of modern human conveniences

Connect the Dots (page 99)

Answers will vary, but the key image must be visible.

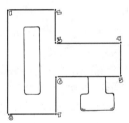

The Best Choice (page 100)

1. a
2. d
3. a
4. a

Explanations will vary.

Author Messages (page 101)

Answers will vary.

Name That Theme (page 102)

Story 1: Treat others the way you want to be treated. OR You never know when you may need the help of someone you hurt.

Story 2: You never know who could

be your best friends. OR Bravery pays off in many unpredictable ways.

Story 3: Treat others the way you want to be treated. OR Kind words go farther than mean words.

Topic or Theme? (page 103)

1. topic
2. topic
3. theme
4. topic
5. theme
6. topic
7. topic
8. theme
9. topic
10. theme
11. theme
12. topic
13. topic
14. theme
15. theme

The explanation should discuss how a topic is generally one word, but a theme is a complete sentence or thought with a subject and a verb.

Poetry (page 104)

1. c
2. e
3. a
4. d
5. b

Type of poem: limerick

Features of Literature (page 105)

usually about animals (fables)

has a moral to share (fables)

passed down through generations (folktales)

originally not written down (folktales)

often has a character that plays tricks on others (folktales)

is usually short and to the point (folktales)

usually involves ancient gods and goddesses (myths)

often includes supernatural powers (myths)

started with the Ancient Greeks (myths)

attempts to explain the mysteries of the world (myths)

involves heroes (legends)

involves superhuman powers or events (legends)

pure fiction (folktales)

no particular place in time or space (folktales)

a story from the past about a historical person (legend)

a sacred story from the past about the universe or life (myth)

Lear's Limericks (page 106)

Answers will vary. Possible answers include:

1. funny—a man running up and down a hill in a nightgown
2. funny—woman made use of malformation and plays harp with chin
3. surprised—the man was sleeping while the rats came in and chewed up his clothes
4. funny but sorry for her—she sat down and tore her dress on a thorn

Positively Poetic (page 107)

1. a bird
2. Answers will vary.
3. Answers will vary.
4. Images will vary.

Sort It Out (page 108)

Herbivores—eat grains and grasses; eat continuously; includes sheep, horses, rabbits, snails

Carnivores—eat meat for energy; don't eat continuously because they can store food for long periods of time; predators in the wild; include wolves, cheetahs, eagles, and dragonflies

Omnivores—eat both plants and animals; includes chickens and chimpanzees

Get Organized (page 109)

Answers will vary.

Catch Phrases (page 110)

Answers will vary.

Acronyms (page 111)

1. SWAT—Special Weapons and Tactics
2. PTA—Parent Teacher Association
3. NATO—North Atlantic Treaty Organization
4. NASA—National Aeronautics & Space Administration
5. FDA—Food and Drug Administration
6. FBI—Federal Bureau of Investigation
7. NBA—National Basketball Association
8. CIA—Central Intelligence Agency
9. CDC—Centers for Disease Control
10. NYSE—New York Stock Exchange
11. DMV—Department of Motor Vehicles
12. FCC—Federal Communications Commission
13. ATV—All Terrain Vehicle

14. USDA—United States Department of Agriculture
15. UN—United Nations

Name That Activity (page 112)

1. f
2. h
3. i
4. o
5. a
6. q
7. k
8. t
9. s
10. d
11. l
12. n
13. r
14. c
15. j
16. p
17. b
18. g
19. m
20. e

What Do You Think? (page 113)

1. The snowstorm was the worst in ten years.
2. He was primarily concerned with the safety of the vehicle.
3. He was a locksmith.
4. It was a pig.

Cartoon Capers (page 114)

Answers will vary. Possible answers include:

Where?—at school

Who?—a student

How?—He did not study for the test.

Why?—He is worried because he is afraid of what his parents will say.

When?—After he received his test paper back from the teacher.

What?—He got a D on his test.

Favorite Sports (page 115)

Pauli—tennis

Bob—soccer

Deanne—basketball

Paul—volleyball

What's Next? (page 116)

Answers will vary.